SEVEN
ESSENTIAL
RELATIONSHIPS

How To Pass GOD's Crucial Tests

Howard Katz

SEVEN
ESSENTIAL
RELATIONSHIPS
How To Pass GOD's Crucial Tests

BELIEVE BOOKS
WASHINGTON, DC

SEVEN ESSENTIAL RELATIONSHIPS
By Howard Katz

All Scripture quotations, unless otherwise indicated, are taken from The Holy Bible, New King James Version, © 1982, published by Thomas Nelson.

Scripture quotations identified as THE AMPLIFIED BIBLE are taken from The Amplified Bible, © 1987, published by The Zondervan Corporation.

Scripture quotations identified as THE MESSAGE are taken from The Message Translation of the Bible, © 1993, published by NavPress Publishing Group.

Scripture quotations identified as NIV are taken from the New International Version of the Bible, © 1984, published by Zondervan.

Scripture quotations identified as NLV are taken from The Bible – New Life Version, published by Barbour Publishers.

Scripture quotations identified as Young's Literal Translation are taken from Young's Literal Translation of the Bible, © 2005, published by Greater Truth Publishers.

Scripture quotations identified as PHILLIPS TRANSLATION are taken from The New Testament in Modern English, © 1995, published by Simon & Schuster Publishers.

The Scripture quotation identified as THE LIVING BIBLE is taken from The Living Bible, ©1971, published by Tyndale House publishers.

Strong, James The exhaustive concordance of the Bible: Electronic Edition (1996).

ISBN: 0-6151582-5-0

Library of Congress Control Number: 2007936916

Cover and layout design: *Jack Kotowicz, Washington, DC, VelocityDesignGroup.com*

Believe Books publishes the inspirational life stories of extraordinary believers in God from around the world. Requests for information should be addressed to **Believe Books** at www.believebooks.com. **Believe Books** is a registered trade name of **Believe Books, LLC** of Washington, D.C.

Printed in the United States of America

To my beloved wife, Lena, the greatest support God could have given me. Your love and faithfulness have sustained me like a refreshing fountain through my most difficult times. You have made marriage such a joyful experience. I look forward to all that God has for us in the future.

And to my brother, Harvey—truly God could not have given me a better brother. Thank you for all your love and encouragement. God has so intertwined our lives together—at work, at church—even on family holidays. And to think we both have authored books. I pray that God will use our lives and our writings for His glory,

CONTENTS

FOREWORD

Seven Essential Relationships stands out from today's crowded marketplace of feel-good, sugar-coated, easy-sell products on bookstore shelves. Compared to the shallow stuff coming out lately, it feels almost quaint at times...a bit like reading one of those Puritan classics, but without the "olde" English.

Howard Katz didn't write this book like he was cramming for final exams. This is the result of decades of learning intimacy with God at a depth few know about these days.

From the life of Joseph, Howard reminds us that there are no short-cuts to really knowing God. Most of it is learned in the school of hard knocks.

The author brilliantly interweaves the vivid metaphor of the potter and the clay—an image that will make this book stick in your brain ten years from now.

This is one of those books you shouldn't rush through. And it's one of those rare books you'll find yourself picking up and reading again as a reference, especially when you go through one of those Joseph experiences.

This book cuts like a scalpel. But thankfully, Howard provides an anesthetic of humor throughout, while he presses ahead with open heart surgery.

I've known Howard for two decades. He walks the talk. As a businessman and a pastor he lives in the real world. In this important book Howard Katz cuts to the chase and gives us the real deal.

WAYNE HILSDEN
Senior Pastor, King of Kings Community,
Jerusalem

ACKNOWLEDGEMENTS

I would like to thank Irina Radchenko and Mary Haskett for their valuable contributions in the initial editing of this manuscript.

A special thank you to Elizabeth Stalcup, Ph. D. for her inspired suggestion to include personal testimonies.

Many thanks also to Eleazar Mendoza for his friendship and many valuable suggestions regarding the content of this book.

Also a special thanks to Daniel Moser for his spiritual guidance.

And last but not least, I am deeply indebted to Shirley Howson for her tireless efforts to help me take what was once a series of teaching tapes and turn these thoughts into a book. Her astute writing and editing abilities were indispensable and her creativity, insights, and wonderful additions have shaped this book. Without Shirley's input and encouragement, this book would never have become a reality.

PREFACE

When I first made a commitment to put my faith in Jesus as my Savior, I was filled with tremendous joy. This joy, however, was mixed with uncertainty and anxiety, as I dreaded having to tell my family—especially my father—about my new faith in Christ. To understand the depth of my reluctance, let me share my family background. First, we are Jewish, and although not strictly observant Jews, being Jewish has always been very important to our family. Second, my father was a Holocaust survivor. Most of my father's family were killed in the Holocaust. My father spent nearly five years in forced labor camps in Hungary and Austria, as well as in the Mauthausen Concentration Camp in Austria, where he was finally liberated—barely surviving with his life. All his suffering occurred for one reason alone—he was Jewish. In my father's mind, receiving Christ would be the same as renouncing my identity as a Jew and turning my back on all the suffering of the Jewish people over the millennia.

When I received Christ I felt the exact opposite. I felt a *greater* identity with being Jewish because at last the God of Abraham, Isaac, and Jacob was real to me, and I had now come to know the promised Messiah—Jesus of the tribe of Judah, born in Bethlehem.

We are a close family and my father dearly loved me. But I knew the shame and shock he would experience when I told him of my faith in Jesus Christ—not to mention the shame and shock I would experience. Despite our close relationship, I understood my revelation would cause a change that would be painful for us both. My faith in Christ would make no sense to him and would cause him a profound sense of betrayal and disgrace. So for a number of months I kept my newfound faith secret.

One Sunday evening, I was at a friend's house where we were praying and sharing about the things of God. I began to share about how I felt I was faltering in my new walk of faith. As I spoke, it occurred to me that the fear and shame that prevented me from telling my father about my faith in Jesus was also sapping my spiritual strength. My lack of resolve to follow Jesus no matter what had produced double mindedness in me. Once I had been excited about the Lord, but now I was beginning to stagnate. I knew that unless I stepped out in obedience and shared honestly with my father, at the same time accepting in my own heart the transformation that had occurred, my spiritual lukewarmness would continue. I shared my situation with my friends and we prayed together. I decided to tell my father that very evening.

I felt a sick feeling in the pit of my stomach. As I drove home I prayed and was hoping that the Lord would help by placing an angel with a flaming sword in the middle of the living room or some other dramatic manifestation. When I arrived home there was no angel or flaming sword—just my dad sitting in front of the TV in his boxer shorts watching the eleven o'clock news. I sat down and began to watch the news but my thoughts were filled with how I was going to tell him. I thought, *I'll tell him after the news.* When the news was finished I thought, *I'll tell him after the weather report before the sports.* After the weather report my father got up to shut the TV off since he was not a sports fan. As he began to walk out of the living room I knew I had to say something or I would put it off for the rest of my life . . .

As I stood before my father that evening in the midst of the intense internal struggle I was experiencing, little did I realize that I was facing one of God's crucial tests, the outcome of which would have a profound impact on the direction of my life. It was only many years later that I would understand the vital importance of passing that test if I were ever to progress in my walk of faith. This book shares with the reader some of what I have learned over the years about the essence of our relationship with God and the crucial tests that He places across our path. The circumstances of each person's life will be different, but the seven essential relationships in which God tests us are the same. I pray this book will be a blessing to each and every reader.

INTRODUCTION

I am indebted to my late friend, Robert Ewing of Texas, for his teachings on the seven types of relationship we have with God. He shared these principles with me shortly after I met him in 1993, but he had received the original revelation many years before I met him. Apparently while he was praying one day, the Lord stirred him to examine the process by which an ancient Israelite potter fashioned a clay vessel. Robert discovered that there were seven steps involved. As he continued to pray and study the Word, the Lord began to reveal to him how each of the steps in forming a clay vessel correlate with seven key relationships that God uses to make us into a vessel for His glory.

Each relationship builds on the previous ones—they are all interlinked. Since these relationships are progressive in nature, one cannot skip one relationship before moving on to the next relationship. God is the Master Potter who works the clay and moves it from one stage to the next. If we fail to respond we can spend a lot of time in the initial stages as a lump of clay, and never move on to spiritual maturity to become a vessel formed and fashioned into Jesus' image. As we advance through the different relationships, from time to time the Lord will take us back to earlier ones to deepen our commitment and strengthen our foundation, so that a more profound relationship with the Lord can be developed.

The Bible uses the visual illustration of the potter and clay to help us clearly understand our relationship with God. Through the eyes of faith we can see evidence of God's unseen hand guiding and directing apparent random circumstances in our life to bring about His purposes. Our part is to be a co-laborer and cooperate with what He is doing.

Meeting Robert Ewing was to me evidence of God's sovereign hand in my life. The Lord is not only a Master Potter but a Master Weaver, who weaves together the apparent smallest threads of life into a beautiful tapestry. God used Robert Ewing as a beautiful thread to change the direction of my life.

This is an example of how God weaves together His tapestry and every once in a while He allows us to see some of the threads come together, and the glorious pattern that they form. God brings together the most exacting details to carry out His purposes in our lives—and this book, which I have chosen to call *Seven Essential Relationships*, is the fruit of the unique teaching that Robert shared with me.

A few years after Robert shared this teaching with me I was sitting in a church waiting for the service to begin. As I sat there I opened my Bible at random and began to read. My Bible opened in Genesis— right at the story of Joseph. As I read the passage, I immediately saw that Joseph entered into the seven relationships in the same chronology that Robert had noted. In the space of fifteen or twenty minutes I found all seven relationships. I became very excited and quickly scribbled some notes on a scrap of paper. I was so encouraged that in the following weeks I began to teach these *Seven Essential Relationships* at Bible study. By the time I finished, thirty-one weeks had passed.

Almost ten years have elapsed since I completed that thirty-one week study and just recently I felt stirred to summarize and document the teaching in written form, incorporating personal testimonies into each section to illustrate how each essential relationship was established in my life, or in the lives of others. I have tried to share my heart and how through my struggles God has been faithful to continue to lead me by His grace through each one of these seven essential relationships.

God has a purpose and a plan for all of our lives to transform us into the image of Jesus Christ, but we need to submit to the process to become a vessel of glory and honor. To grow spiritually, we need to understand that producing a vessel of glory is not all God's responsibility, neither is it all our responsibility. God desires that we respond to Him with willingness and obedience as He leads us through the seven essential relationships. As we grow spiritually in our Christian life, we need to pass tests in each of the seven relationships to be molded into the vessel God created us to be and to fulfill His calling on our lives.

Often in times of struggle or discouragement, I have referred back to this teaching to discover what essential relationship God was working on and how I was being prepared to pass the accompanying test. This has helped me refocus on the eternal perspective and to cooperate with the work the Holy Spirit was doing, and to apply this teaching to my own life. My prayer is that the Lord will use this book to inspire you to become a vessel of glory shaped by the Master's hand.

OUR RELATIONSHIP WITH GOD'S WORD
The Obedience Test

Our first relationship is with the Word of God and it is the most primary and essential relationship that we have as Christians. The test that we must pass in response to God's Word is the obedience test.

When an ancient Israelite potter wanted to create a clay vessel, he would first go to a place where clay was found and dig it from the earth. This removal from the earth, this separation of the clay from the dirt, is a picture of what happens when we repent and receive the Lord Jesus Christ as Savior. We have a new life and identity in Christ and we no longer belong to this world. *"Dear friends, your real home is not here on earth. You are strangers here."* (1 Peter 2:11, NLV). The Apostle Paul tells us that we *"...sit together in the heavenly places in Christ Jesus..."* (Ephesians 2:6), and further elaborated on that thought, saying *"...our citizenship is in heaven..."* (Philippians 3:20). We are clearly *in* the world, but no longer *of* it. Both our identity and residency have changed.

At the moment we receive Christ, our identity changes, and we are no longer a part of this world and its sinful life. We are redeemed, we cease to be children of darkness, and we become children of light— children of God. When we hear the Gospel, the Word of God, the first thing we have to do is respond in obedience to the Word.

THE THREE WASHINGS

After the clay was dug from the earth, it was washed in a number of basins to remove any excess dirt and impurities that clung to it. There are three washings in our Christian walk—the first two are one time occurrences and the third is a continuous process. Each of the three washings has one commonality—it requires a step of obedience on our part.

We see the first washing, the washing of regeneration in Titus 3:5, *"...not by works of righteousness which we have done, but according to His mercy He saved us, through the washing of regeneration and renewing of the Holy Spirit..."* This initial washing occurred at the moment of our salvation, when we received the Word, obeyed it, and received Christ.

The second washing is another step of obedience which is accomplished by partaking in water baptism. After we receive the Lord Jesus and have been saved, God tells us to be water baptized (Mark 16:16). We are not saved through water baptism but it is a step of obedience to God's Word, signifying that we want to be His disciples.

The third washing is the daily washing so beautifully described in Ephesians 5:26, which says, *"...that He might sanctify and cleanse her* (the church) *with the washing of water by the word..."* (Insertion mine). This washing is provided by our daily relationship with the Word of God. As we live in this sinful world, we often become contaminated and we need a daily washing in the Word of God. That means not only reading the Word—it means having a relationship with, and being obedient to, the Word of God. Some people claim that they read the Bible every day, but fail to see any improvement in their lives, insisting that they still feel the same. But the question is this: "Are they obedient to what they are reading?" The Bible does not tell us to read the Word of God day and night, but to meditate upon it day and night, indicating that something more than simply reading it needs to happen.

RELATING TO GOD'S WORD

The Bible gives us a clear and proper view of God and how we are to relate to Him. God tells us who He is in His Word. Isaiah and Job are but two books in the Bible that expound on God's character, but all of Scripture reveals the essence of God—who He is, what He does, what He loves, and what He hates. If we do not have a deep relationship with God's Word we will have a distorted or incomplete view of God, causing a shallow or false relationship with Him.

His Word is one of the most precious gifts God has given us. In countries where the Bible is banned or severely restricted, believers there know it to be precious, and hang on to every word. Many in the West take it for granted and fail to count it as precious and in fact treat it with neglect. We need to live just as Jesus said, *"not by bread alone but by every Word that proceeds from the mouth of God."* Revelation of the Word of God brings life. As we read, study, and meditate upon God's Word the Holy Spirit deepens and quickens our intimacy with God, as He reveals His true character.

Our relationship with the Word of God is not restricted to times when we are actually reading it; His Word is also activated when we pray, worship, and fellowship—even during our daily activities. *His Word should be our constant companion.*

We can enjoy a relationship with His Word as we worship God, with the truth of Who He is foremost in our thoughts. It may be His love, mercy, awesome power, or holiness—whatever aspect of God that causes our hearts to become filled with praise, awe, and worship. The Bible shows us God's attributes and we cultivate that revelation in meditation, in worship, and even through fellowship as we share with one another the awesome things of God.

When we feel overwhelmed, it indicates that our view of God is incomplete or distorted and we lack faith in God's sovereignty and provision. But *"...faith comes by hearing, and hearing by the Word of*

God." (Romans 10:17). The solution is to worship Him for His all powerful sovereignty and unlimited provision for our lives. As we meditate on those truths from God's Word and worship Him, our image of God will grow and mature. One of the reasons worship is so important is because our ability to trust Him will increase. Unless we devote time to worshipping God, our image of God will not grow.

Israel thought they were serving the God of Abraham, Isaac, and Jacob but in fact they had a distorted view of God. Solomon began to serve idols as he bowed down to pieces of wood and stone, for he had lost his revelation of God. Israel sought help from other sources besides God because their view of God was not big enough. As Christians we often have a false image of God—that our God is not big enough. Sometimes believers seek the ways of the world because they are not convinced that God's ways work. They look to the world for pleasure because they do not believe that in His presence is fullness of joy. Their view of God lacks both the joy and the power that He truly possesses. It is through His Word that the Holy Spirit imparts to us the correct image of God and worshipping God in spirit and truth restores a correct view of God.

PRAYING GOD'S WORD

Prayer is another way in which we relate to God's Word. The Lord used a prophetic brother named Harold to help me to understand how the Word of God relates to prayer. In the spring of 1994, as I was praying with Harold and some friends, I began to earnestly pray and plead with God to save souls. I was pleading and begging God to move by His Spirit so that many would be saved. When we finished praying, Harold looked at me and said, "The way you pray really tickles me." I was taken aback by his comment. If he had said, "Your prayer really moved me or really touched me," I could understand that, but when he said my prayer really tickled him I felt a little embarrassed. But Harold continued, "I asked the Lord, 'Why does Howard pray that way?' and the Lord said, 'He just doesn't know any better.'" At this point I felt a little insecure. I didn't really understand what he was referring to so I asked him what he meant. He looked at me with his big friendly Texas grin and said, "Oh, just the way you were pleading with God to save souls. You don't have to plead with God to save souls. He wants to save people more than you could ever begin to imagine. That is like someone pleading with me to eat ice cream." And I could tell by his girth that Harold enjoyed eating ice cream. He added, "Your heart was right but your understanding was wrong."

So I asked him how I should pray. (Remember I had already been a believer for almost eighteen years and it was a shock for someone to suddenly tell me that I didn't know how to pray.) He gave me a very simple but profound piece of advice that changed the tone and content of my prayer life. He asked, "Have you ever heard Robert Ewing pray? Much of what he prays is patterned after the Word of God." During the next few days I listened more carefully to Robert's prayers. His prayers were filled with faith and with confessions of God's faithfulness. He would speak forth God's Word in prayer and declare the goodness of God. As he lifted up the needs of others he would declare with thanksgiving God's willingness and faithfulness to bless and to answer exceeding abundantly above all that we could ask or think. Robert's prayers contained no place of hesitation or questioning of God's intentions—He believed that God not only would do good—He would do the very best.

Later I mentioned to Robert that I noticed that his prayers were filled with Scripture. His response was interesting. He smiled and said he had never really thought about that before. His prayer life was not the result of trying to mechanically recite or parrot Scripture, but because his heart was so filled with the Word of God that it spontaneously poured out of him in prayer. There is great power in praying God's Word. Isaiah 55:11 says, *"So shall My word be that goes forth from My mouth; it shall not return to Me void, but it shall accomplish what I please, and it shall prosper in the thing for which I sent it."* If we discern God's heart for a situation and apply the appropriate Scripture in prayer, we know we are praying His perfect will for that person or situation.

From that time on I too began to base my prayer life on the truth found in God's Word, and very quickly a greater power and authority began to be manifest in my communion with God.

JOSEPH'S RELATIONSHIP WITH GOD'S WORD

Joseph was the elder of two sons born to Jacob by his union with his beloved Rebekah. Rebekah was *"...beautiful of form and appearance..."* and Jacob served Laban for fourteen years to obtain her hand in marriage (Genesis 29:18-28). God changed Jacob's name to Israel, and gave him powerful promises. *"And God said to him, 'Your name is Jacob; your name shall not be called Jacob anymore, but Israel shall be your name.' So He called his name Israel. Also God said to him: 'I am God Almighty. Be fruitful and multiply; a nation and a company of nations shall proceed from you, and kings shall come from your body. The land which I gave Abraham and Isaac I give to you; and to your descendants after you I give this land.'"* (Genesis 35:10-12). This story illustrates how God used Joseph to fulfill the promises He had given to Jacob, his father.

How do we see this relationship with the Word of God lived out in the life of Joseph? Genesis 37, beginning at verse five, describes two dreams that Joseph had. In the first dream Joseph saw himself with his brothers and they were binding sheaves. As they bound the sheaves, Joseph's sheaf arose and stood, and his brothers' sheaves all bowed down to his sheaf. Joseph told his brothers about his dream and his brothers, who already envied Joseph because of his special relationship with their father, Jacob, now hated and despised him even more for having what they considered a boastful attitude.

Joseph had a second dream in which he saw the sun, the moon, and the stars all bowing down to him. When he told his brothers and his father, his father rebuked him saying, *"Shall your mother and I and your brothers indeed come to bow down to the earth before you?"* (Genesis 37:10b). Although Jacob, Joseph's father, rebuked him for his attitude, he kept in mind the words that Joseph had spoken. Jacob recognized that God had spoken prophetically to Joseph in a dream, and that this word *was* indeed from God. Although Joseph's attitude was less than one of total humility and may have contained some element of self-centeredness, he valued the Word that God had given him.

When God speaks His calling into our lives, we may tend to think it is because we are important, but that is not God's reason for placing a calling on our lives. God's calling on our lives is evidence of His goodness and grace and is not based on our righteousness or self-importance. As we receive God's Word and respond to it, it will expose areas in our hearts that need to be dealt with so that God can fulfill His Word in us. Many times we can be tempted to treat God's Word as undesirable when it produces hardship or conflict. Joseph however, valued the Word of God even though it caused great conflict in his family.

One day Joseph's father said to him, *"Are not your brothers feeding the flock in Shechem? Come, I will send you to them."* (Genesis 37:13). Joseph responded with obedience when he said to his father, *"Here I am."* Joseph knew obedience—he knew obedience to his father and he knew obedience to the Word of God, evidence that Joseph's first essential relationship with God had been established.

There are many Christians today who are not obedient to God's Word, although it is the foundational relationship. The Word of God contains many clear instructions which if applied and obeyed, will be a conduit for the release of God's grace in our lives. Jesus said in Luke 11:28, *"...blessed are those who hear the word of God and keep it!"* The Word of God is so much more than a list of "do" and "don'ts"; rather it is a book of revelation that teaches us how to live in the Spirit, free from the bondage of sin.

Once, as others and I were praying for someone, a person in our group had a vision in which he saw a lump of clay. As soon as I heard the vision, I felt I knew what it meant—that the person we were praying for was a Christian who had failed to obey God's Word and was still struggling with the first and most fundamental relationship.

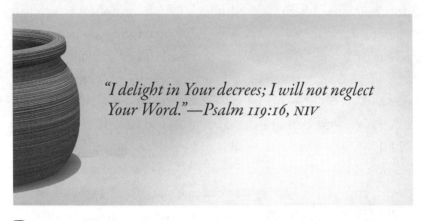

"I delight in Your decrees; I will not neglect Your Word."—Psalm 119:16, NIV

Passing the obedience test means coming to a place of full obedience. Partial or delayed obedience may be seen as a type of disobedience if one continues in that place. Partial obedience can be a stepping stone to full obedience, but partial obedience may also be an indication of double mindedness, perhaps leading to spiritual stagnation, lukewarmness, bondage, and ultimately a backslidden condition. We as believers are at times challenged by God to bring us to a greater degree of obedience to His Word and to the leading of the Holy Spirit.

One of the most profound changes in my Christian life happened when I was 37 years old and had been a believer for seventeen years. At this time in my life I was married and had three sons, I had a career and I consistently went to church and prayer meetings. On occasion I even gave short sermonettes in church. However, there was an area where I was not obedient. It was in the area of my personal devotional life, where the problem was not so much rebellion as neglect.

My typical day began by getting out of bed and making my way to the front door. I opened the door just enough to extract the morning newspaper from my mail box. It must have been comical for passersby to see a pajama-ed arm reach out the front door each morning as if by clockwork. Stumbling to the kitchen, I read the newspaper while I ate breakfast. By the time I finished breakfast there was just enough time to get dressed and drive to work. I spent the day dealing with all my responsibilities at work. When I arrived back home I ate dinner and then lay down to rest for a few minutes. Sometimes I read a scientific magazine or some other related topic. Then I worked around the house or went out. By the end of the evening I was dead tired. I would get ready for bed and while lying in bed, I would pull out the Bible and try to read. Very shortly I began to nod off. It is difficult to read the Bible with one eye closed—you can only read half the page! My total time spent reading the Bible and praying probably amounted to about five minutes, and the quality of that time was quite poor.

Even though I felt badly about it, resolving that the *next* day would be different, this pattern continued for many years. I lacked both obedience and the power to be obedient.

Then one Sunday night we had a prayer meeting at church. While praying, there was a prophecy to "read the book of Malachi." Even though the prophecy was directed toward the whole group I felt a special stirring. At home after the prayer meeting, I sat in the living room and read the book of Malachi. These verses from Malachi 1:6-8 really jumped out at me.

"A son honors his father, and a servant his master. If then I am the Father, where is My honor? And if I am a Master, where is My reverence? Says the Lord of hosts to you priests who despise My name. Yet you say, 'In what way have we despised Your name?' "You offer defiled food on My altar, but say, 'In what way have we defiled You?' By saying 'The table of the Lord is contemptible.' And when you offer the blind as a sacrifice, is it not evil? And when you offer the lame and sick, is it not evil? Offer it then to your governor! Would he be pleased with you? Would he accept you favorably?' says the Lord of hosts."

As I read those three verses my conscience was convicted as I realized that I was despising the Lord by my attitude. I had given Him the sacrifice of the blind, the lame, and of the sick. How was I doing that? I did not give the Lord my quality time when I was fresh, but my leftover time at the end of the day when I was exhausted. After I understood those verses, I prayed and acknowledged that I had sinned and asked the Lord to help me to change. Yet the next morning when I awoke, I did what I had done for many years. I went to the front door, stuck my hand into the mailbox and retrieved the newspaper. I followed the same pattern for the duration of the week. Even though my desire was to change and obey, I lacked God's grace and His empowerment for it to be accomplished.

During the prayer meeting the next Sunday night, the pastor asked if I had anything to share from the Bible before we began to pray. I read the verses from Malachi—the very verses that had touched me so deeply the week before. Then I said, *"Who is not guilty of this?"* By "this" I meant robbing God by not giving Him the best of our time and energy. I repeated the question a second time. Suddenly a very strong presence of God literally enveloped me. My eyes were closed and I felt a blanket of cool air surrounding me. The room and the people seemed distant. My body began to tremble uncontrollably like a thousand volts of electricity were passing through me as I continued to ask, "Who is not guilty of this?" By this time I was no longer in control of what I was saying, but the Holy Spirit was speaking the words through me. I did not feel a terror but I definitely felt a powerful reverence of God filling me and I was in awe at what was happening. I fell to my knees and with my eyes still closed I began to shout to the Lord, "I have sinned and treated You with contempt." As I continued to pray out loud and confess my sins I ceased to care what people thought about me because the reality of God's presence was so tangible. I did not feel God was angry with me. Instead I was overwhelmed with the reality that He loved me so much that He would personally visit me in such a powerful way.

While this was happening the people in the room were awestruck as they watched me. One minute I was reading the Scriptures and the next I was on my knees confessing my sins and being physically shaken by the power of the Holy Spirit. Suddenly someone said, "What are *we* doing? We need to pray too." Then everyone fell on their knees and began to pray and repent.

As I drove home after the prayer meeting, I was really excited about the Lord and what He had done. The next morning when I awoke I took my Bible and went into my study and began to read and pray. From that day God changed my devotional life. I began to become a man of prayer.

Reflecting back, I see that God wanted me to move forward in my spiritual walk where for many years I was hindered because of an area of disobedience. Regardless of how many church services I went to or how many prayer meetings I attended I could only go so far in my Christian walk. God wanted obedience in my personal devotional life. *He wanted me to have a relationship with His Word.* There may be areas where we are disobedient to the Lord and because of our disobedience we are at a spiritual standstill, unable to move forward, and perhaps precariously close to moving backward. Until we pass the obedience test with God's Word we will be limited in our spiritual growth.

Passing the obedience test sometimes requires several steps. First I had to recognize the area in which I was disobedient; second, I needed to choose to be willing to change; third, I had to pursue God so that I could receive the grace that He wanted to impart to me; and fourth, I had to obey, pick up my Bible and resist the habit of reaching for the newspaper. If we make the decision, God will empower us to carry out our obedience.

Heavenly Father, forgive me for those areas in my life where I have failed to value, revere, and obey Your Word. I am unable to change without Your grace. Empower me by the power of Your Holy Spirit and the life of Your Son, Jesus Christ within me to fully obey Your Word from the depth of my heart. I want to love and fully embrace Your Word. Thank You Lord that You are faithful to lead me to a place of complete obedience. Amen.

Our Relationship with the World
The Separation Test

The second essential relationship is our relationship with the world, and the test we must pass is the separation test. How is this relationship illustrated in the picture of the ancient potter and the clay? After the clay was washed it would be too wet to be used, so the potter would place the clay on the side of a hill where exposure to the sunshine and wind would dry it to a workable consistency. This step in the formation of a clay vessel represents our relationship with the world.

For Christians there are two aspects to our relationship with the world. The first aspect is recorded in Matthew 5:14-16, in which Jesus says, *"You are the light of the world. A city that is set on a hill cannot be hidden. Nor do they light a lamp and put it under a basket, but on a lampstand, and it gives light to all who are in the house. Let your light so shine before men, that they may see your good works and glorify your Father in heaven."* In other words, one of the purposes of our relationship with God is to be a light to the world. Some Christians believe that to serve God they need to enter a monastery and dedicate themselves to God by isolating themselves from every temptation. But that response contradicts Scripture. The Bible says we *shouldn't* put our light under a basket; we should be a light to the world.

The second aspect of our relationship with the world is presented in John 16:33: *"These things I have spoken to you, that in Me you may have peace. In the world you will have tribulation; but be of good cheer, I have overcome the world."* The Amplified Bible phrases it this way, *"I have told you these things, so that in Me you may have [perfect] peace and confidence. In the world you have tribulation and trials and distress and frustration; but be of good cheer [take courage; be confident, certain, undaunted]! For I have overcome the world. [I have deprived it of power to harm you and have conquered it for you.]"* We see that in our relationship with the world we're going to have tribulations and troubles, that's a reality! But God has a divine purpose for our tribulations and troubles.

Washing the clay made it too wet to be used immediately. As a new Christian I remember hearing the Word of God and learning about the Lord, and I thought, *Praise the Lord! I'm so excited about God—I'm going to be a super Christian! I'll read all those Scriptures and just fulfill them. It's so easy! Why aren't others living a victorious life for Jesus?* But I was still too wet; the Word was all theoretical. It is our relationship with the world that takes the theoretical and makes it a reality. As a young Christian, for example, when I read, "Love your enemies," I thought, *Oh yes Lord, I'm going to love my enemies.* But there is one very important thing we need if we are going to love our enemies—we need *enemies*! Until someone has hurt us, until someone has defiled us, or wronged us, we cannot love them as our enemies because the Word of God is only theoretical in our minds and lives. We need to grasp the reality that we require the grace of God to love our enemies. When we feel the pain of betrayal, of people doing malicious things to us, only then does the Word of God become real. We may try to act like super-spiritual Christians but we are without any real context of experience. The difficult reality of having enemies gives us a context of experience in which we can examine our hearts.

Obedience is not based on our ability to perform something, but on our willingness to be obedient. If we have the correct attitude, we will respond by saying, "I'm willing." Initially we may not love our enemies, but through our willingness to be obedient, God can take us to the next step where He teaches us how to forgive those who harm us, how to overcome evil with good, how to love our enemies, and how to do good as a consequence of our relationship with His Word and with the world.

Jesus spoke of our separation from the world in His prayer for believers in John 17:14-16: *"I have given them Your word; and the world has hated them because they are not of the world, just as I am not of the world. I do not pray that You should take them out of the world, but that You should keep them from the evil one. They are not of the world, just as I am not of the world."*

John carefully instructed the church in the following passage: *"Do not love the world or the things in the world. If anyone loves the world, the love of the Father is not in him. For all that is in the world—the lust of the flesh, the lust of the eyes, and the pride of life—is not of the Father but is of the world. And the world is passing away, and the lust of it; but he who does the will of God abides forever."* (1 John 2:15-17). Paul also wrote about our separation from the world. Second Corinthians 6:16-17 says: *"And what agreement has the temple of God with idols? For you are the temple of the living God. As God has said: 'I will dwell in them and walk among them. I will be their God, and they shall be My people. Therefore come out from among them and be separate, says the Lord. Do not touch what is unclean, and I will receive you.'"*

Some Christians believe that the only way to live a holy life is to isolate themselves from the world. Jesus did not pray that God would take us out of the world; rather He prayed that God would keep us from things that would defile our lives while we're in the world. For example, the society in which we live is filled with pornography. It can be seen on billboards, in the media, in movies, on television—it is everywhere. But God does not want us to leave this country; rather He wants us by His grace to make godly choices about what we read, what we look at, and to govern our thoughts. God wants us to have contact with unbelievers, but He wants us to learn not to be defiled by that contact. The separation test distinguishes us from the world.

THE SEPARATION TEST IN JOSEPH'S LIFE

How do we see the separation test applied to Joseph's life? Joseph's father, Jacob, asked Joseph to go and see how his brothers were doing. And Joseph obeyed as he responded, *"Here I am."* In obeying his father Joseph ultimately obeyed God. *Obedience to God's Word always brings about the separation test.*

"Now Israel (Jacob) loved Joseph more than all his children, because he was the son of his old age. Also he made him a tunic of many colors. But when his brothers saw that their father loved him more than all his brothers, they hated him and could not speak peaceably to him." (Genesis 37:3-4).

In Genesis 37:18 we read, *"Now when they saw him afar off, even before he came near them, they conspired against him to kill him."* Joseph innocently walked toward his brothers, unaware of their evil intent. *"Then they said to one another, 'Look, this dreamer is coming! Come therefore, let us now kill him and cast him into some pit; and we shall say, "Some wild beast has devoured him." We shall see what will become of his dreams!'"* (Genesis 37:19-20). But Reuben intervened and instead of killing Joseph they threw him into a pit and later sold him into slavery. Why did Joseph's brothers despise him so much? Certainly they were jealous because he was his father's favorite and the most loved. His brothers also despised Joseph because he unashamedly held to the Word of God that came to him though dreams revealing aspects of his future. At the age of seventeen Joseph became separated from his father, his brothers, his home, and his country. Joseph's separation from his family was not of his choosing but a result of his obedience to God's Word. The very dreams that God gave to Joseph and the value

Joseph placed upon those revelations from God caused Joseph's brothers' hostility toward him to become inflamed.

When Joseph's brothers decided to sell him as a slave, they also devised a scheme to explain Joseph's disappearance to their father. *"So they took Joseph's tunic, killed a kid of the goats, and dipped the tunic in the blood. Then they sent the tunic of many colors, and they brought it to their father and said, 'We have found this. Do you know whether it is your son's tunic or not?' And he recognized it and said, 'It is my son's tunic. A wild beast has devoured him. Without doubt Joseph is torn to pieces.'"* (Genesis 37:31-33).

Jacob saw Joseph's tunic with the goat's blood on it and concluded that Joseph was dead. When we receive the Lord Jesus Christ and begin to walk with God and allow the blood of Jesus to be applied to our lives, others will look at us. They will see the blood and conclude that we are dead, that they no longer know us. They will wonder, *Where is the fellow who used to party, the one who told dirty jokes?*

As believers our first step in passing the separation test is our willingness to be obedient to God's Word. As we begin—step by step—to obey what God is showing us, our way of life changes. As we begin to make godly choices, wholesomeness enters our soul. This wholesomeness heals and brings greater stability into our soul, enabling us to be more obedient and make even more godly choices. This cycle of *willingness* to obey by exercising our faith, releases grace so we are *able* to obey—and that releases healing which brings a greater wholesomeness in our souls, so we are willing to take larger steps of obedience.

It is for this reason that when troubled people with many problems and bondages come to Christ, initially the Lord only requires them to deal with one or two seemingly minor issues. However, as the person obeys, greater healing and grace to deal with the larger problems is released. We see an interesting interaction between obedience and sanctification. The more obedient we are—the more our lives are filled with godly things—the more healing and sanctification occurs.

The more sanctification and healing that take place in our soul, the more obedient we will be, and we will be empowered to make even more godly choices.

When we first come to Christ with all our hurts, bondages, and rebellion, what should we do? We need to fall at the feet of Jesus, submit to His grace, mercy, and love, and allow His Holy Spirit to lead us through the process that brings us to a place of obedience, sanctification, and freedom. Our first step of obedience may be as simple as being willing to receive His love.

The separation test is really a work in our hearts that causes changes in how we relate to the world around us. Temptations that once drew us like a magnet lose their grip as we submit to the leading of the Spirit and we are instead drawn to godliness.

Our obedience to God by choosing godly things and shunning evil will produce two contradictory effects in our lives. First it will bring a deep satisfaction. Matthew 5:6 says, *"Blessed are those who hunger and thirst for righteousness, for they shall be filled."* The second thing it will produce is persecution and rejection as stated in Matthew 5:10-12: *[10] "Blessed are those who are persecuted for righteousness' sake, For theirs is the kingdom of heaven. [11] Blessed are you when they revile and persecute you, and say all kinds of evil against you falsely for My sake. [12] Rejoice and be exceedingly glad, for great is your reward in heaven, for so they persecuted the prophets who were before you."*

Not all of us will experience the violence of persecution, but we can experience persecution in milder degrees as people may snub, reject, or mock us. When we stand for righteousness, we may be labeled as closed minded, bigoted, or even prejudiced. As we take our stand for Jesus, we may experience social tensions at work, at school, with our neighbors—even in our own homes. While not endangering our lives, these tensions do put pressure on our souls that can be very uncomfortable and emotionally painful.

God wants to use even adverse circumstances to bring a depth of joy that comes only from the Spirit. He also wants to use those adverse circumstances to proclaim the Gospel to the world. Separation from the world may cost us a few friends but it will also be used to win many souls to Christ.

Some unbelievers may no longer want to be around us. Our interests and motivations will have changed and others can no longer identify with us. Even respectfully living non-Christians may become agitated with us as our thoughts, desires, and conversation reflect a more heavenly tone. They'll remind us of all the fun things we used to do. But we have changed and we no longer want to live the same way. We are not refusing to be around non-Christians, but we are beginning a new way of living. Our changed lives will convict them of their own sins, and will either cause them to want to hear the Gospel, or cause them to despise us. They will react to our obedience to God's Word, and they'll be either drawn to God or offended.

The Message translation describes our changed life this way: *"Your old life is dead. Your new life, which is your real life—even though invisible to spectators—is with Christ in God. He is your life. When Christ (your real life, remember) shows up again on this earth, you'll show up, too—the real you, the glorious you."* (Colossians 3:3-4a). If we pass the separation test, one of the effects it will ultimately have on our souls is to bring a true joy that is not rooted in the circumstances of this life but in the salvation that we have in Christ. It may take many years before this joy becomes a reality, but when it does, it becomes one of the signs of a true disciple of Christ.

"Anyone who loves his father or mother more than Me is not worthy of Me..."
—*Matthew 10:37a, NIV*

"Therefore come out from them and be separate, says the Lord."
—*2 Corinthians 6:17a, NIV*

Shortly after I received Christ, I discovered to my surprise that my brother Harvey had put his faith in Christ a few months earlier. So my younger brother, who is four years younger than me, was four months older than me in the faith! One day my brother approached my father and told him that he believed Jesus was the Messiah. This was a huge step for Harvey as our family is Jewish. Our father was a Holocaust survivor who made sure we were brought up in the religion and traditions of our people, even sending Harvey to a private Hebrew day school. My father was disturbed at Harvey's views yet not especially upset since Harvey was only sixteen years old. My father thought he was easily influenced and this was only a passing phase. He had a back up plan—me—or so he thought. He felt that as the older brother I could easily straighten out Harvey. One day while I was in the bathroom brushing my teeth my father came in to inform me of the situation with Harvey. He asked for my input.

I almost swallowed my toothbrush! My father wanted me to convince Harvey to stop following the "Christian faith" and smarten up. I didn't know what to do. I was still too afraid to tell him about my faith in Christ but at the same time I did not want to deny the One in Whom I had placed my faith. I wasn't yet ready to pass the separation test—at least not while cornered in the bathroom. I knew there was only one thing to do—*keep brushing my teeth!* That toothbrush prevented me from making incriminating or perjurous statements. Eventually my father tired of the one-way conversation and left the bathroom. I certainly had clean teeth that day!

During the next month or so, I was able to avoid the topic of my brother's faith. But as the weeks passed, I noticed that my spiritual growth began to stall. Unlike the first few months of my new faith in Christ where I grew rapidly and had a great hunger to know more about the Lord, I felt I had hit a spiritual wall. I continued to fellowship and pray with other believers but now something was not quite right. As I shared in the preface to this book, I realized that unless I stepped out in obedience and shared honestly with my father, my spiritually stagnant condition would continue.

The moment had come—I could not put if off any longer. This was the evening I would tell my father that I had accepted the Lord Jesus Christ as my Savior. My friends and I had prayed that evening, and I could no longer endure my own spiritual procrastination. I knew that my life would never be the same when I accepted the Lord—now it seemed my life would never be the same when I told my father. How would the events of my life unfold? I had no idea where my new faith in Christ would take me. Once my declaration of faith was spoken, it could never be taken back. Pushing past the fear, I took a deep breath and said, "I want to talk to you about something." My father quickly turned around and with great interest sat down beside me and giving me his full attention asked, "Did you find out who has been influencing Harvey?"

The tension I felt was incredible because I both loved and respected my father but I wanted to honor and obey my Savior and God. My profession of faith in response to my father was "I believe it too." Not what you would call a great bold statement of faith in the Lord Jesus, but it conveyed the idea clearly enough.

His shock, disbelief, and anger erupted almost immediately. I was overwhelmed by my dad's response and wept as he was overcome by his own pain at my revelation. Later I learned that my brother was in his bedroom with the covers pulled over his head wishing to be invisible. This first encounter lasted probably less than an hour but it felt like an entire night. No one slept well that night but somehow relief and peace filled my heart.

My spiritual journey was back on track. My obedience to God by confessing my faith caused a profound and abrupt change in my relationship with my father but in time God restored our relationship. The separation test was not that I chose to reject my father—on the contrary—I wanted to have an honest relationship with him, which meant I needed to be open with him about my relationship with Christ. Many years passed and slowly, with reluctance, my father came to accept my faith in Jesus Christ. My brother and I continued to pray for our father's salvation. Three years before he passed away, he too received the salvation that can only be found through faith in Jesus Christ.

Heavenly Father, I thank You for the wonderful salvation You have given me through Your Son, Jesus Christ. Make me a witness of Your grace to all those around me. Let not self-consciousness or the fear of man hinder me to be that light but give me a sensitivity to Your Holy Spirit to know when and what to share. As I press through the trials of this life, purify my heart and empower me so that my response will be godly and will glorify Jesus. I want to be used by You to see many come to a saving knowledge of Jesus, to be turned from the path of darkness to the path of eternal life. Amen.

OUR RELATIONSHIP WITH AUTHORITY
The Submission Test

Our third essential relationship with God is our relationship with authority and the corresponding test is the submission test. When the ancient potter would take the clay from the earth it would be inconsistent in texture. To produce an even texture, the potter had to place it on a rock or a hard surface, and step on it with his feet. As he stepped on the clay, he would find some areas too stiff and some too soft. The potter would continue to work the clay with his feet until it formed a homogeneous consistency—entirely uniform throughout. This represents our relationship to authority and the submission test. Once the clay becomes consistent and pliable, it can be molded to the shape of the potter's foot without resistance. Any hard portions in the clay are like pressure points and the clay would feel the stamp of the potter's foot. These areas represent stubbornness and rebellion in our souls. Our desire is to do it *our* way. When we have such attitudes, we will not respect authority; we will feel the pressure of authority because of our stubbornness. So the Master Potter works the clay until those stubborn areas are softened and we learn submission. Our submission protects us from rebellion and from being self-willed, and from the harmful consequences these traits produce in our lives.

Jesus is our Potter. His feet were pierced for us. When there are hard spots of rebellion within us, not only do we feel the pressure, but the Potter's feet also experience the pain of our rebellion and stubbornness. Jesus suffers with us. His heart grieves over wrong attitudes in our hearts, but He never gives up on us, and continues to work to soften those hardened areas. Jesus' feet can be compared to the five-fold ministry: those apostles, prophets, evangelists, pastors, and teachers that our Lord has provided for the equipping and edification of the Church. (Ephesians 4:11-12). Those ministering in the five-fold ministry are used by God to apply pressure to areas of hardness within our hearts. Just as Jesus' heart grieves for us, those ministering must do so with compassion.

OBEDIENCE AND DISOBEDIENCE VERSUS SUBMISSION AND REBELLION

We need to appreciate what submission is because it is a concept that many Christians do not understand. They wonder how they should respond if a person in authority tells them to do something wrong. We need to understand four words: obedience and disobedience, submission and rebellion. Obedience and disobedience are outward actions, while submission and rebellion are inward attitudes. It is entirely possible to be submissive and at the same time disobedient. For example, if a husband asks his wife to help him rob a bank, no one would suggest his wife should think, *Well—he's my husband—I guess I should do what he says.* That would be a false assumption because the husband's command clearly contradicts the Word of God. Since submission is an inward attitude, a woman can disobey her husband while still honoring him if what he is asking her to do is wrong.

SUBMISSION TO GOVERNMENTAL AUTHORITY

Paul tells us that God installed governments, and there is no authority that God has not established. *"Let every soul be subject to the gov-*

erning authorities. For there is no authority except from God, and the authorities that exist are appointed by God. Therefore whoever resists the authority resists the ordinance of God, and those who resist will bring judgment on themselves." (Romans 13:1-2). God allows unrighteous governments to take office and we need to honor even their authority. However, that does not mean that we always have to obey them. For example if they said, "Don't go to church, don't have fellowship, don't read the Bible, and don't share the Gospel," we could disobey, but still honor the government. Christians have often misunderstood this, especially in the United States, but also in other countries, including Canada. People often speak in ways that dishonor the government. But our dishonoring words are not in keeping with Paul's admonition in Acts 23:5: *"Do not speak evil about the ruler of your people."* (NIV). We can disagree with the government's actions, but we need to do so with respect rather than personally attacking those in leadership in a vindictive way.

The test that accompanies our relationship with authority is the submission test. Our relationship with the Word is tested by our obedience, but our relationship with authority requires a greater degree of maturity and commitment to Christ. Submission is a deeper issue than obedience because it is the result of the attitude in our hearts.

THREE ASPECTS OF SUBMISSION TO AUTHORITY IN JOSEPH'S LIFE

During the next stage of Joseph's development when he was a lived as a slave in the house of Potiphar, we observe his three separate encounters with authority:

SUBMISSION WHEN AUTHORITY IS FAVORABLE

The first aspect of submission to authority is when the authority is favorable to us. Joseph was unrighteously sold as a slave into the house of Potiphar, a very important man in Egypt. Because he submitted to his master's authority, God's hand of blessing was upon Joseph. Potiphar recognized the blessing upon Joseph and, as his home prospered, made him head servant over his entire household, allowing him some liberty and authority although Joseph remained a slave. Joseph could have become bitter and said, "It's not fair! I'm *not* a slave. I'm a free man unrighteously sold into slavery." But he recognized that God's hand had placed him in the situation, so he chose to honor his master, and in return he was treated with respect.

There are many Christians who refuse to submit to authority even when the authority is favorable to them. I recall meeting a Christian who told me his story with pride. His pastor asked him, "How is everything going? Maybe you could come to the prayer meeting on Sunday?" The man answered, "I don't go *anywhere* unless *I* want to." He could have said, "Well, I appreciate your invitation and I'll pray about it." But he displayed an attitude of opposition, resistance, and rebellion to the pastor who was reaching out to him. He was really saying, "I don't need anybody and I don't have to listen to anybody." He refused to submit even to a favorable authority.

SUBMISSION WITH THE RIGHT ATTITUDE AND MOTIVATION

The second aspect of our relationship with authority is submitting to authority with the right attitude and motivation. This relationship with authority is seen in Joseph's life as he served his master. When Potiphar's wife began to notice Joseph in a sensual way and wanted to commit adultery with him, Joseph's response is recorded in Genesis 39:8-9: *"But he refused and said to his master's wife, 'Look, my master does not know what is with me in the house, and he has committed all that he has to my hand. There is no one greater in this house than I, nor has he kept back anything from me but you, because you are his wife. How then can I do this great wickedness, and sin against God?'"*

In Joseph we see genuine honor and submission to Potiphar's authority. Joseph knew it would be disgraceful and sinful to sleep with his master's wife. Joseph honored Potiphar from his heart, and not for selfish gain. He submitted to Potiphar with the right attitude and pure motivation. If Joseph had wished to be vindictive, he could have slept with his master's wife, but he refused to do such a thing. Joseph chose instead to honor both God and Potiphar.

Some people want to have a good relationship with those in authority because of personal ambition. They do not really care about the authority, but only want to be close to their boss or pastor, because it will somehow benefit them. They are not truly submitted, and their motivation reflects self-promotion. Their actions appear to be correct but their underlying attitude is wrong. True submission desires to bless those whom God has placed in authority.

This story illustrates the difference between obedience and disobedience, submission and rebellion, attitude and motivation. A little boy had misbehaved. His mother told him to sit down in the corner and be quiet. But the little boy said, "I'm not going to the corner, and I'm not going to sit down or be quiet." The mother said, "If you don't go in that corner and sit down, then when your papa comes home he's going to use the wooden spoon on you." So the little boy went to the corner, sat down and said, *"I may be sitting down on the outside, but I'm standing up on the inside!"* Outwardly he was obedient, but his sole motivation was to avoid punishment, and his attitude remained one of rebellion.

God does not want to confine Himself to dealing with just our outward actions or our motivation. He wants to go right to the heart of the matter and correct our attitude. A correct attitude will bring about correct motivation which in turn will change our outward actions. *Attitude always supersedes motivation—if our attitude is correct, our motivation will be as well.*

SUBMISSION WHEN AUTHORITY IS UNFAVORABLE

The third relationship to authority is the most difficult because it occurs when an authority figure treats us unjustly or unrighteously. Potiphar's wife continually tried to seduce Joseph and one day as he ran from her, she grabbed his clothes. She felt so humiliated and angry by Joseph's refusal to sleep with her that she told Potiphar's men that Joseph had tried to rape her. When Potiphar returned home she told him, and Potiphar, in a rage, threw Joseph into prison. Although Joseph had been a long-time and faithful servant, when this terrible accusation came, Potiphar denied Joseph the opportunity to defend himself, and unjustly threw him into prison without any hope of release. Potiphar probably suspected that his wife was not totally truthful, but rather than face that reality, he chose to place the blame exclusively on Joseph.

Despite this despicable treatment by an unfavorable authority, Joseph honored Potiphar. We can presume this because God prospered Joseph while he remained in prison. If we have unresolved issues from the past, God cannot bless us because bitterness will contaminate our relationship with everyone around us and with God. But Joseph overcame any bitterness he may have harbored.

Potiphar could not help but fulfill the will of God for Joseph's life because Joseph submitted to his authority. It was not God's will for Joseph to be the highest ranking servant in Potiphar's home—instead it was God's will for Joseph to rule over Egypt and to be the savior of Israel. Joseph continued to believe in the sovereignty of God and refused to believe that the will of man could thwart the purposes of God.

THE EXAMPLE OF SHADRACH, MESHACH, AND ABED-NEGO

I love the story of the three Hebrew men, Shadrach, Meshach, and Abed-Nego as told in the third chapter of the book of Daniel. King Nebuchadnezzar built a large golden statue which he commanded all the people in his kingdom to worship. He decreed that if the people did not fall down and worship the statue, they would be thrown into the midst of a fiery furnace. Daniel 3:12 tells us that the three Hebrew men, who were in a position of some authority in the kingdom, refused to bow down to a false god. The king flew into a rage when this was reported to him and he summoned them to appear before him.

King Nebuchadnezzar said, *"Is it true, Shadrach, Meshach, and Abed-Nego, that you do not serve my gods or worship the gold image which I have set up? But if you do not worship, you shall be cast immediately into the midst of a burning fiery furnace."* (Daniel 3:14,15b). Note their response: *"If that is the case, our God whom we serve is able to deliver us from the burning fiery furnace, and He will deliver us from your hand, O king. But if not, let it be known to you, O king, that we do not serve your gods, nor will we worship the gold image which you have set up."* (Daniel 3:17-18). Their submissive attitude is clearly shown in these two verses as they twice referred to Nebuchadnezzar as "O king." They honored his position of authority, but they refused to worship his gods. The young men risked being thrown into the furnace without any assurance that God would save them. They respected Nebuchadnezzar's position as their king while refusing to obey his commands.

I might have been tempted to say something like, "You're wrong and I'm right. You're going to suffer eternal damnation, and realize that you're nothing! I'll be in the furnace for a few minutes, but you'll be in Hell forever." But they responded with respect: "O king." After they were thrown into the fiery furnace, the king looked in and said, *"Did we not cast three men bound into the midst of the fire? Look! I see four men loose, walking in the midst of the fire; and they are not hurt, and the form of the fourth is like the Son of God."* (Daniel 3:24-25). When he saw this, the king was astonished and called for them to come out of the fiery furnace.

Noticing that the king was visibly shaken by this notable miracle, the three Hebrew men could have been cocky and replied, "Why don't you come in and get us?" But Shadrach, Meshach, and Aded-Nego obeyed God, honored the king, and came out unharmed—not even smelling of smoke. The king responded to their submission and respect for him by promoting them to positions of greater authority in the kingdom. King Nebuchadnezzar also commanded that no one in his kingdom was to speak against their God, saying, *"...because there is no other God who can deliver like this."* (Daniel 3:29b). Shadrach, Meshach, and Aded-Nego had demonstrated their respect for the king, their obedience to God, experienced a miracle of God, and as a result King Nebuchadnezzar now honored their God.

I believe the king promoted them not only because they were miraculously saved from the fire, but with greater reason because they honored him even in his wrongdoing. If they had disgraced him and lived, he probably would have isolated them in a distant part of his kingdom, preventing them from speaking with anyone, for fear they would incite rebellion. King Nebuchadnezzar saw that they were able to speak up, but they did so respectfully, honoring him and the position God had given him. The story of Shadrach, Meshach, and Aded-Nego clearly shows that their actions resulted from obedience to God —they honored kingly authority while disobeying his command— their action was motivated by the right heart attitude.

THE DIVINE IRONY OF CAIAPHAS' UNFAVORABLE AUTHORITY

Caiaphas is another example of an unfavorable authority fulfilling God's will. John 11:49-51 says, *"And one of them, Caiaphas, being high priest that year, said to them, 'You know nothing at all, nor do you consider that it is expedient for us that one man should die for the people, and not that the whole nation should perish.' Now this he did not say on his own authority; but being high priest that year he prophesied that Jesus would die for the nation."* Caiaphas in fact prophesied that it was God's will that Jesus would die so the nation of Israel would not perish.

Caiaphas, the high priest, motivated by jealousy, displayed an envious heart toward Jesus. But because of his position as a high priest, an anointing of authority rested on him. Although motivated entirely by defiled thoughts and desires, Caiaphas could not help but fulfill the will of God for the Lord Jesus. The Father was able to use Caiaphas to fulfill His will and plan for Jesus' life even though Caiaphas was unrighteous in his thoughts and actions, because Jesus submitted to his authority as high priest. Not only did Caiaphas prophesy Christ's atoning death, but in God's divine irony he also prophesied Christ's resurrection.

Leviticus 23:5-11 speaks about two celebrations that are intertwined: the first is the Passover and the second is the celebration of the Barley Harvest, also called the first of the firstfruits as seen in Exodus 23:19 and 34:26. In Israel, barley was planted in the autumn and harvested in the springtime, making it the firstfruits of the grain harvest, maturing before the wheat harvest. Leviticus 23:10-11 instructs the people to bring barley sheaves and give them to the high priest. The priest waved these sheaves before the Lord as the new day began after the Sabbath had ended. I believe that this Sabbath was the end of the weekly Sabbath during the week in which the Passover had taken place. Biblically the new day begins not at sunrise but at sunset.

First Corinthians 15:20 reveals the significance of this ritual by referring to Jesus as the "firstfruits of those who have fallen asleep." *"But now Christ is risen from the dead, and has become the firstfruits of those who have fallen asleep. For since by man came death, by Man also came the resurrection of the dead. For as in Adam all die, even so in Christ all shall be made alive. But each one in his own order: Christ the firstfruits, afterward those who are Christ's at His coming."* (1 Corinthians 15:20-23). The prophetic picture painted is of the resurrection of Jesus Christ from the dead and of those who believe in His name at the time of His return.

At what time of day then did Jesus' resurrection occur? John 20:1 describes how Mary Magdalene went to the tomb while it was still dark, by which time the tomb was *already empty*, because Jesus *had already been resurrected!* Christ's resurrection occurred not at sunrise, but sometime after sunset! I believe that after sunset, as the Sabbath day came to an end and the sky was growing dark—as the first day of the week was beginning—at that very moment Caiaphas was waving the sheaves of barley gathered by the people of Israel, before the Lord. At the very moment the high priest was unwittingly prophesying the resurrection of Christ—*at that very moment*—Jesus, our High Priest was coming forth from the tomb. Caiaphas' prophetic act and Jesus' fulfillment of that prophecy occurred simultaneously. As Caiaphas waved the firstfruits before God, God resurrected His Firstfruits, His Son Jesus. Christ's resurrection prepared the way for the resurrection of all who place their faith in Him.

But perhaps the greatest irony is found in Matthew 27:62-66. After Jesus' crucifixion, His body was given to Joseph from Arimathea by Pilate to be prepared for burial. The next day the chief priests and the Pharisees led by Caiaphas went to Pilate and reminded him of Christ's promise to rise on the third day. They asked that the tomb be secured, the stone sealed, and guards set around, so His body could not be stolen and to prevent Jesus' disciples from feigning His resurrection. Pilot's response was one of disinterest and almost mocking in tone: *"You have a guard; go your way, make it as secure as you know how."* Caiaphas not only established a secure guard around the tomb, but sealed it. His actions actually helped to validate Christ's resurrection by providing eye witnesses to the event. The crowning touch was that while Caiaphas was prophetically waving the barley sheaves before the Lord proclaiming symbolically the resurrection of Jesus Christ, the very seal he had set on the tomb was being broken and his own guards, charged with protecting the tomb, were frozen with fear at the appearance of the resurrected Christ.

God used Caiaphas in the dual role of both archenemy of Jesus and high priest to plot and prophesy both His death and resurrection, demonstrating God's sovereign hand as He uses even unrighteous and unfavorable authorities to fulfill His ultimate purposes.

When we submit to authority—regardless of whether that authority is favorably disposed toward us or not—and with the right heart attitude—we are entering into God's plan to fulfill His purposes in our life. In God's divine order, there is a positive correlation between obedience and submission, and promotion within His kingdom. This is clearly seen in the lives of the three Hebrew men, in Joseph's life, and in Jesus' life. Shadrach, Meshach, and Aded-Nego submitted to an unrighteous authority—Nebuchadnezzar; Joseph submitted to Potiphar; while the Lord Jesus honored and did not disdain an unrighteous spiritual authority—the high priest Caiaphas. Because they submitted to unrighteous authority, they were all promoted to positions of *greater* authority. *God promotes people who are willing to submit to authority to be in authority.* When our inward attitude agrees with our outward actions, God will work the situation for our good and for His glory, and the authority of Christ in us will be manifest.

Joseph passed the submission test when the authorities God placed over him were both favorable and unfavorable, as he responded with the right motivation and attitude in each case. As Joseph learned to submit from the heart, it placed him in a position where God could deal with deeper issues of his soul in the subsequent essential relationships. Joseph learned through his relationship with authority to accept God's direction for his life—no matter where or how it led him—to reach God's intended destination. God cannot lead us into a deeper relationship until we are fully willing to submit to His will, no matter if the path is smooth or very difficult.

"Be responsive to your pastoral leaders. Listen to their counsel. They are alert to the condition of your lives and work under the strict supervision of God. Contribute to the joy of their leadership, not its drudgery. Why would you want to make things harder for them?"
—Hebrews 13:17; THE MESSAGE

God used the third essential relationship, the relationship with authority, to set me free from the bondage of legalism. This occurred at a point in my life when I had been a believer for seventeen years. I was following Jesus and had a genuine desire to serve the Lord but I was steeped in legalism. My concept of serving God was going to church three or four times a week and acting very proper and serious during the services. I had many rules by which I measured myself and others. Though many of my standards had a sound moral basis, they produced in me a sense of both self-righteousness and self-condemnation. I had a sense of self-righteousness as I looked down on others who did not measure up to my standards, while I continued to struggle with internal issues in my heart which produced self-condemnation.

The Lord used a minister of the Gospel to set me free from this bondage and put me back on the path of growing in His grace. The first time I met Robert Ewing I immediately judged him in my heart. He did not belong to the denomination I belonged to and he seemed unnaturally relaxed and carefree. He was in his late sixties when I met him and he was totally unpretentious—a truly humble and generous man of God. But my legalism distorted my view of him and I saw him as proud and a teacher of false doctrine. My self-righteousness made me suspicious of anyone who did not believe exactly what I believed. At first I kept quiet and just observed him. From my legalistic point of view I did not recognize the true characteristics of Christ within him. Little did I know that this man was going to be the very person that God would use to do a wonderful work of grace in my heart. Although he had an apostolic ministry and had traveled to many nations to minister to churches and individuals, the Lord sent him to me to set me free.

During our first encounter Robert immediately discerned my suspicious and legalistic attitudes. His response was to pour out love and acceptance toward me. We didn't meet again until a year later, yet I later learned that throughout that time he continued to pray for me. By the time we met the second time my heart had begun to change. I sensed that something was missing in my relationship with the Lord. I had not found the great intimacy and freedom for which I hungered. This time I was more open to what Robert had to share. As we prayed together the Lord gave him a prophetic word for me that really touched my heart. It produced within me an expectation that God was going to move in a special way in my life. A few weeks later the Lord visited me in a very wonderful way. My relationship with God began to blossom. As I spent more and more time with the Lord, it occurred to me that Robert Ewing had something to teach me that I desperately needed. I began to realize that there was something very godly and Christ-like about him. I called him and asked if I could visit him at his home in Texas. He agreed. A month later I spent six days with him studying the Word of God, day and night. Hour upon hour, he opened the Word of God to me and I took copious notes. God had given him many deep revelations from the Word which he meticulously shared with me. I began to see the amazing grace of God in ways I never imagined. My heart began to be filled with faith and joy.

Over the next year I often spoke with Robert by telephone. I visited him a couple of times in Texas and he came to Canada to visit me. It was a wonderful time! He was becoming a spiritual father to me. His care and spiritual support really nurtured me in my relationship with the Lord.

One day Robert phoned me and asked if I would accompany him on a mission trip to Romania. He felt it would be beneficial to my spiritual walk and that I could be a blessing there as well. As soon as I heard his invitation I immediately knew the answer was "no." I didn't see how I could be of any help to him and I couldn't see any benefit for myself. I had a young family. I thought, *Why would a nice Jewish boy like me go to a place like Romania? Wasn't that one of the countries that used to persecute Jews and Christian believers?* I told Robert I would pray about it but felt of course I already knew the answer. A few days later I went to a prayer meeting. No one at the prayer meeting knew why I was seeking the Lord. During the prayer meeting there was a prophecy directed toward me. The answer the Lord gave me was really surprising. The prophecy was very simple: "I have given you a faithful man, now submit to him." The people I was praying with knew nothing about my situation or my relationship with Robert. The answer was profound and suggested a much greater commitment than simply making an overseas trip. As soon as I heard the prophecy, its truth resonated in my heart. The Lord had not just provided me with a good friend but a spiritual father and mentor as well. Right then I decided to submit to God's choice of who was to oversee my spiritual life.

I went to Romania with Robert. The trip had a profound impact on my spiritual life. As I traveled with Robert and observed his walk with the Lord and how the Lord ministered through him, I began to grow in my relationship with Christ. We also spent valuable time together praying and studying God's Word.

God used Robert to speak into my life and bring the preciousness of accountability, until the Lord took him home eight years later. Through my relationship with Robert, I developed an understanding of how to submit to authority and how God uses authority to lead and shape us. If I had not passed the submission test some very precious things would have been lost or lacking in my life. After Robert's homegoing, the Lord provided other men of God to whom I would be accountable. Through accountability God has kept me from straying, provided encouragement during difficult times, and given me godly counsel as to the Lord's will for the difficult decisions and challenges in my life. I never feel isolated or hopeless—even in the most difficult situations. God's wonderful provision of the five-fold ministry—apostles, prophets, evangelists, pastors, and teachers—has been not only a blessing, but a safeguard.

Heavenly Father, thank You for those whom You have placed in authority in my life. Give me a heart that is submissive, humble, and seeks only to glorify Jesus Christ. Help me to honor and pray for those in authority over me and to recognize it is You who placed them in my life. Teach me to value those in authority and to receive what I need from them that I may continue to grow in the grace and purposes of God. Thank You for godly authority that You use to provide protection and guidance for my life. Amen.

THE WAY IN WHICH GOD DEALS WITH US
The Preparation Test

The fourth essential relationship is with the way in which God deals with us and the accompanying test is one of preparation. When the clay became evenly consistent and malleable, the ancient potter pulled a wire taut and cut the clay in half to expose its inner parts. If any air bubbles or defects were present, he put the clay back together, and pounded it with a mallet to remove the air. This was a critical step because if the air bubbles were not removed before the formed clay vessel was placed into the kiln to be fired, the heat would cause the air bubbles to expand and the vessel would be ruined. Many of the air bubbles hidden in the clay would be small and may have appeared insignificant to the untrained eye, but in the heat of the kiln those small pockets of air greatly expanded with disastrous results. Any flaws in the preparation of the vessel hindered it from being completed and becoming a vessel of glory fit for the master's use.

When God is beginning to deal with our hearts, we may feel that the issues He is exposing are not that important and if left alone would never cause problems. We may think, *I have that area of temptation under control.* But later when we are exposed to fiery trials or God's glory those small areas of temptation quickly expand and grow out of control—and suddenly what we once considered a minor character flaw wreaks havoc in our life.

For this reason the preparation test is very important as God deals with the deepest, inner issues of our heart. One of the attitudes the air bubbles can represent is pride. We may not even realize we have pride, but when the glory of God touches us, unless we have dealt with our pride, we will take some of the glory for ourselves, blow up like a balloon and explode in a burst of self-destruction. We have often seen people who were powerfully used by God who self-destructed because of pride, their life left in shambles. Pride causes a person to be unteachable and incapable of receiving correction. When God prospers us and our ministry becomes successful, we need to be especially humble, open to correction, and watchful to avoid the snares of the enemy. God wants to rid us of our defects and He squashes the "air bubbles" in us as He does a deeper work within our hearts. When God exposes the pride within us, and our plans or sense of self-importance are deflated, we may experience discouragement. In this way, pride and discouragement are related. Pride causes us to become puffed up with a sense of self-importance. If we fail to deal with the hidden areas in our hearts when God exposes them, those areas will cause destruction and much discouragement later.

Often we are unaware of our own flaws. There were no obvious faults in the clay either; only when the potter cut it open did the flaws become visible. When flaws are revealed in us we think, *Whoops, there's an attitude I didn't know was there!* Our natural tendency is to blame others for our defects instead of dealing with the sin and wrong attitudes within our own hearts. The preparation test prepares us for the things that God has planned for us in the future. We should not resist the way in which God deals with us but welcome and embrace it even if at the time it causes us great pain or humiliation. We should respond to God immediately and deal with our sin as God reveals it—before it expands in the fire and blows up in our face as a much bigger problem than if we had dealt with it earlier.

Even as the Lord admonished His people in Psalm 81:13-14: *"Oh, that My people would listen to Me, That Israel would walk in My ways! I would soon subdue their enemies, And turn My hand against their adversaries."* The process of our deliverance from sin and bondage slows down or speeds up depending upon our response to the way in which God deals with our personal lives. This preparation protects us from hidden failures, weakness, or sin in our souls which would surface in the future when God wants to use us in ministry.

RELATING TO GOD'S PERSONAL DEALINGS

We may question how we can have a relationship with an abstract concept like the way in which God deals with us or what I call "God's Personal Dealings." It is much easier to envision a relationship with the Word of God, with the world, or with authority, but how can we have a relationship with God's Personal Dealings? Like any relationship, it is important how we interact and relate to God's dealings in our particular circumstances. When we are going through trials we can either view them as enemies sent to afflict us, or as friends sent to help us to change.

In The Phillips Translation of the Bible, James speaks of our relationship with adversity so beautifully: *"When all kinds of trials and temptations crowd into your lives, my brothers, don't resent them as intruders, but welcome them as friends! Realise that they come to test your faith and to produce in you the quality of endurance. But let the process go on until that endurance is fully developed, and you will find you have become men of mature character, men of integrity with no weak spots."* (James 1:2-4).

The Bible does not say that all things are good. But God weaves together both the pleasant and tragic circumstances of our lives to make a beautiful tapestry that brings forth an eternal weight of glory. When God brings about or allows circumstances into our lives that place pressure on our souls, we have to choose how we are going to relate to what is happening. We can react to our circumstances with disappointment, bitterness, anger, or resentment—*or* we can respond to our circumstances by acknowledging the goodness of God and yield to the Lord, allowing Him to work His nature in us through adversity.

GOD WORKS ALL THINGS TOGETHER FOR GOOD

The following passage of Scripture from Romans 8 offers us a road map for dealing with adversity, trials, and temptations. It illustrates the purpose of our trials and provides encouragement for the journey.

> [28]*And we know that all things work together for good to those who love God, to those who are the called according to His purpose.* [29]*For whom He foreknew, He also predestined to be conformed to the image of His Son, that He might be the firstborn among many brethren.* [30]*Moreover whom He predestined, these He also called; whom He called, these He also justified; and whom He justified, these He also glorified.* [31]*What then shall we say to these things? If God is for us, who can be against us?* [32]*He who did not spare His own Son, but delivered Him up for us all, how shall He not with Him also freely give us all things?* [33]*Who shall bring a charge against God's elect? It is God who justifies.* [34]*Who is he who condemns? It is Christ who died, and furthermore is also risen, who is even at the right hand of God, who also makes intercession for us.* [35]*Who shall separate us from the love of Christ? Shall tribulation, or distress, or persecution, or famine, or nakedness, or peril, or sword?* [36]*As it is written: "For Your sake we are killed all day long; We are accounted as sheep for the slaughter."* [37]*Yet*

in all these things we are more than conquerors through Him
who loved us. [38]For I am persuaded that neither death nor life,
nor angels nor principalities nor powers, nor things present nor
things to come, [39]nor height nor depth, nor any other created
thing, shall be able to separate us from the love of God which is
in Christ Jesus our Lord.—Romans 8:28-39

Verse 28 reveals a great truth about the sovereign purposes of God but there are certain qualifications that must be satisfied for this promise to become a reality in our lives. First it says, *"And we know that all things work together for good."* Do we know this is the truth—not only in our heads but deep in our hearts? We must be convinced of this truth to view our life experiences with eyes filled with hope and faith. Perhaps we are filled with negative expectations from our past experiences with other people. The question very much becomes, "Do we believe *in* God or do we believe *God Himself?*" The second qualification is: *"to those who love God."* For this to become a reality we must not be self-seeking or self-centered, but be motivated by our love for God. The third point this verse makes is: *"to those who are the called according to His purpose."* This is an invitation given by God to each of His children to enter into His divine purpose for their lives. Notice that the word *purpose* is singular—there is only one purpose—to be conformed to the image of Jesus. If we seek only our plans and purposes, we will easily become disheartened when our plans do not come to fruition, but when we embrace God's purpose we will experience fulfillment.

We must have an awareness of God's definition of *good*. Without the correct definition we will be unable to respond correctly. We may be resisting the very things that the Lord wants to do in our heart. Verse 29 defines for us the proper definition of *"working together for good,"* by saying that God's purpose is that we are *"to be conformed to the image of His Son." Good* is not necessarily being successful in the eyes of this world, living a comfortable life, or seeing all our dreams come together the way we thought. "Working together for good" means we are to be shaped and molded into the unchangeable image of Jesus Christ.

The Greek word *conformed* does not mean just a resemblance, or a changeable or unstable image, but one that is durable and is the essence of the character of the object that is the prototype. *Our prototype is the Lord Jesus!* Many times we try to look and act like Jesus but we lack character in the depth of our soul. In some circumstances we act in a godly fashion but at other times our thoughts, words, and actions reveal sin that has yet to be dealt with in the depths of our heart. The Father's desire is to conform us into the image of His Son, to the very depth of our being. Paul expresses God's desire for complete purification: *"Now may the God of peace Himself sanctify you completely; and may your whole spirit, soul, and body be preserved blameless at the coming of our Lord Jesus Christ."* (1 Thessalonians 5:23). And what a precious promise the following verse contains: *"He who calls you is faithful, who also will do it."*

Verse 30 speaks about predestination, calling, justification, and ultimately our glorification. This indicates that there is a process required for this conformation to become a reality.

Verse 31 makes an interesting statement which may almost seem out of place with the previous text: *"What then shall we say to these things? If God is for us, who can be against us?"* A similar idea is repeated in verse 33: *"Who shall bring a charge against God's elect? It is God who justifies."* Verse 34 continues this thought, *"Who is he who condemns? It is Christ who died, and furthermore is also risen."* Verse 35 raises a related question: *"Who shall separate us from the love of Christ?"* Why is there an emphasis on our security in Christ directly following these statements about being conformed into the image of Jesus Christ? I believe it is because of the process by which God deals with us. When God begins to weave the circumstance of life together to sanctify our soul so that Jesus can be manifest, sometimes it is very painful when sin and wrong attitudes begin to surface and are exposed. In addition to the pain we are already experiencing, the enemy would want to heap shame, confusion, and condemnation as well. Paul is asking, *"Who can be against us, who can accuse us, who can condemn us, who can separate us from God's love in Christ Jesus?"* The answer is *nothing* and *no one.*

When we respond to the way in which God deals with us, we must not allow the enemy to bring accusation against us, but be convinced in our hearts that *"He who did not spare His own Son, but delivered Him up for us all, how shall He not with Him also freely give us all things?"* (v 32). Verse 34 offers us more encouragement: *"It is Christ who died, and furthermore is also risen, who is even at the right hand of God, who also makes intercession for us."* Not only has the Father given us freely (graciously) all things through His Son, Jesus Christ, and withholds nothing that is good from us, but Jesus is constantly interceding on our behalf even during our times of perceived failure. Often we feel that we're doing well when we're on the mountain top, but more sanctification occurs in the times when we are valley dwellers, when God is dealing with hidden sin, attitudes, or unbelief in our souls. During such times we must face the deep issues of our hearts and be empowered to stand against the shame, condemnation, hopelessness, and sense of abandonment the enemy tries to pour upon us—to know that He will forgive us, and that God is for us and not against us—this is the life of faith and our realization of this truth brings joy to God's heart.

Verse 36 reveals the severity of the circumstances we might face. *"For Your sake we are killed all day long; we are accounted as sheep for the slaughter."* If in the midst of these apparently tragic circumstances, we can be confident of God's faithfulness, we will be conformed into the image of Jesus. The way in which God deals with us can, if we cooperate, bring us to a greater degree of surrender and trust in His faithfulness.

THE PREPARATION TEST IN JOSEPH'S LIFE

Genesis 39:20-21 illustrates God's personal dealings in Joseph's life. *"Then Joseph's master took him and put him into the prison, a place where the king's prisoners were confined. And he was there in the prison. But the Lord was with Joseph and showed him mercy, and He gave him favor in the sight of the keeper of the prison."* Of all the trials Joseph endured, this is the only time in the whole story of Joseph where it states that the Lord extended mercy to him. As Joseph found himself in a prison not of his own making, God was with him, showed mercy, and extended His favor to see him through. Similarly, when God exposes issues in our hearts, He's not saying in a heartless way, "Aha! Have a good look at what is *really* in your heart!" When we see the true condition of *our* hearts, His heart is touched by the sorrow we feel and His hand of mercy is extended toward us. Paul noted this in Romans 2:4, saying, *"Don't you realise that God's kindness is meant to lead you to repentance?"* (PHILLIPS TRANSLATION).

Look at Joseph's experiences: rejection by his brothers who wanted to kill him, sold into slavery, and then treated with terrible injustice by Potiphar, the very man whom he tried so faithfully to serve. We can only presume what thoughts and feelings began to surface in Joseph's heart as he sat in prison. Joseph was likely thinking, *I've tried to be faithful. I honored him more than anyone could ever imagine, and he throws me into prison!* Imagine the issues that Joseph faced: anger, unforgiveness, bitterness, and resentment against his father for sending him to his brothers, against his ten older brothers for selling him into slavery, against Potiphar's wife for her false accusation, against Potiphar for his wrongful imprisonment—perhaps anger and rebellion against even God for allowing these circumstances. But as Joseph battled against unforgiveness, bitterness, and self-righteousness within his heart, the Lord extended mercy to him.

When God exposes the evil in our hearts, we must be aware of God's extension of mercy to us, or we will misinterpret His intentions and be filled with condemnation, shame, and guilt. If we feel condemnation we will either shrink away from God in shame, or be filled with accusation and blame others for the ways we have thought and acted. Just as Joseph became aware of God's hand of mercy extended to him, we must also be aware that God's tender hand of mercy and grace is extended to help us and lift us up in our moments of failure. If we do not become conscious of God's mercy and grace extended to us, we will revert to our old ways of self-protection and continue to say, "No, no, the problem is not *me,* it's this situation. I'm not so bad, after all I'm just human—it's the fault of those *other* people! I'm angry because of what that person did, or I'm discouraged because of what that person said." And all the while it is as if God is saying, "I'm extending mercy to you so the issue can be dealt with and removed. I do not condemn you but wish to free you." In fact, the process is a sign of God's favor and love toward us.

At this stage the clay is meant to be cut and the pieces beaten together repeatedly until all the air bubbles are removed. The clay is beaten to prevent the destruction of the completed vessel in the kiln. In the same way God does not want to do a work in us or through us that will be destroyed in the fire of His glory. First Corinthians 3:12-15 exhorts us to build things that will not be destroyed in the fire of God's judgment—gold, silver, and precious stones, and not wood, hay, and straw which will be consumed in the fire. Both encouragement and incentive are promised in 1 Corinthians 3:14: *"If anyone's work which he has built on it endures, he will receive a reward."*

The work God does in the preparation test is of such quality and excellence that it can pass through the fires of testing without suffering loss or damage. The reward that God desires to impart to each of His children is not the evidence of external accomplishment but rather a heart that is fully dedicated to Jesus. The preparation test reveals God's character in terms of His thoroughness, as the Master Potter notices hidden defects in the clay which would go undetected by an inferior potter. Issues in our heart hidden even from our conscience are carefully exposed and removed by God. His goal is to bring forth a glorious vessel that can withstand the fire of His glory. His heart yearns to share His reward with His children.

Psalm 105:17-20, speaks of Joseph saying, *"He sent a man before them—Joseph—who was sold as a slave. They hurt his feet with fetters, he was laid in irons. Until the time that his word came to pass, the word of the Lord tested him. The king sent and released him, the ruler of the people let him go free."*

Note that it says the Word of the Lord tested Joseph. *"For the Word that God speaks is alive and full of power [making it active, operative, energizing, and effective]; it is sharper than any two-edged sword, penetrating to the dividing line of the breath of life (soul) and [the immortal] spirit, and of joints and marrow [of the deepest parts of our nature], exposing and sifting and analyzing and judging the very thoughts and purposes of the heart."* (Hebrews 4:12; THE AMPLIFIED BIBLE).

Verse 18b says, *"He was laid in irons."* The word *he* in this verse is actually the Hebrew word "soul." Young's Literal Translation renders this verse, *"Iron hath entered his soul,"* while the Darby Translation reads: *"His soul came into irons."* Clearly Joseph was physically restrained—but his soul was also in bondage. This passage of Scripture draws our attention to how much his external circumstances affected Joseph's soul. The word *irons* gives us a beautiful and clear insight into how very painful and difficult this experience was for Joseph, but through his sufferings the Lord was doing a beautiful work. God used adversity to refine his soul and Joseph's suffering provided a fast track to spiritual growth in his life.

Wrong thoughts and wicked intentions lie dormant in our hearts until a person or situation quickens them and the Word of God exposes them. Then we finally realize, "It's *me*, it's not them. They may have problems, but it's *my* heart that is wrong." When we let the Word of God cut us open, then God will start to heal those areas. Through his trials, Joseph had to cling to the Word of God. It is in those times that we wonder how God could ever use someone with a heart like ours. We must continue to believe that God has a plan and that we are yet a work in progress. (Philippians 1:6).

Of all the seven essential relationships, this is probably the most painful one because it deals with the wrong attitudes, motives, and desires in our heart. Jeremiah had it right when he said, *"The heart is deceitful above all things, and desperately wicked; who can know it?"* But his question was answered in the next verse, *"I, the Lord, search the heart."* (Jeremiah 17:9-10a). Often we are unable to discern what is really in our heart and it is through God's personal dealing with us that He exposes the depths of our heart, wrong motives and attitudes that on our own we would be incapable of discerning. David understood this when he asked God, *"Search me, O God, and know my heart; try me, and know my anxieties; and see if there is any wicked way in me, and lead me in the way everlasting."* (Psalm 139:23-24). This process reveals the true character of our heart so that God can cleanse us and conform us to the image of His Son. Throughout this cutting and exposing process, God's hand of compassion and mercy is extended to us.

PETER'S PREPARATION TEST

Before His arrest, Jesus had warned Peter of a preparation test he was about to endure. *"Simon, Simon, Satan has asked to sift you as wheat. But I have prayed for you, Simon, that your faith may not fail. And when you have turned back, strengthen your brothers."* (Luke 22:31-32; NIV). Jesus promised not only to intercede for Peter, He prophesied that Peter would be turned back and restored. He also spoke forth Peter's calling—to strengthen his fellow believers. Jesus did not say, *"if* you are restored," but *"when* you are restored." He left no question—Peter *would* pass the preparation test! Peter had passed the obedience test, the separation test, and the submission test to such an extent that God's grace would enable him not to react with bitterness or rebellion—or to turn his back fully away from God—or to return to his former fleshly pursuits. Instead, when faced with his failure of faith Peter allowed God to do the necessary work in his heart during those agonizing days.

Jesus had cautioned Peter that Satan had asked to sift him like wheat. The word *sift* means "by inward agitation to try one's faith to the verge of overthrow." The phrase *turned back* comes from a root word meaning, "to turn one's self from one's course of conduct." But Peter was filled with such faith and confidence in *himself* that he replied, *"Lord, I am ready to go with you to prison and to death."* (Luke 22:33; NIV). Peter thought his heart was purely devoted to Jesus—he was completely sincere when he made that statement.

Then Jesus prophesied that Peter would deny Him three times. It was not spoken as a rebuke to Peter, but to give Peter revelation about the true condition of his heart. The purpose of the trial that Peter was about to go through was not meant to punish him. God's purpose was to purify and prepare him for his calling so he could be used for the Lord's glory in a much greater way. Peter was unaware that much of his zeal was driven by his own strength of character rather than by the grace of God. Not until he denied Jesus three times and saw the Lord's face looking at him did he realize what he had actually done. Can you imagine the agony, despair, shame, and guilt he must have felt—the inward agitation? Scripture tells us that Peter went outside and wept bitterly. The sharp edge of God's dealings cut Peter deeply to expose the true condition of his heart—*to himself.* For the next three days as Jesus' body lay in the tomb, Peter experienced the agony of seeing who he really was.

Peter was just as much in prison as Joseph was, as he had to face the shame of his own soulish, self-centered confidence. Peter didn't realize it at the time but he had *not* been abandoned by God—in fact the Holy Spirit was doing a deep work in his heart through those excruciatingly painful days. Indeed, after Christ was resurrected Mary was told, *"But go, tell His disciples—and Peter."* (Mark 16:7a). How those words must have encouraged Peter and flooded his heart with joy! Later, there would be other times when Peter would experience the sharp two-edged sword of God exposing his heart. But in this season of his life, he was being adequately prepared to preach the first evangelical message of the Church.

What a sharp contrast between the Peter we see before Jesus' crucifixion with the man we see less than two months later—after the day of Pentecost. Peter had indeed been sifted like wheat—he had passed the preparation test, his faith had not failed, and he was now actively functioning in his calling. As Peter and John ministered together, Peter spoke these words: *"Silver and gold I do not have, but what I do have I give you: In the name of Jesus Christ of Nazareth rise up and walk."* (Acts 3:6). Peter, like Joseph before him, realized that whatever gifts he had been given were not of himself but were from God.

Gone was the head-strong, impulsive, self-reliant Peter. First Peter 1:6b-7 illustrates his spiritual maturity: *"...though now for a little while you may have had to suffer grief in all kinds of trials. These have come so that your faith—of greater worth than gold, which perishes even though refined by fire—may be proved genuine and may result in praise, glory and honor when Jesus Christ is revealed."* Peter, like Joseph, now saw his trials from an eternal perspective—that his own faith had been refined by the fire of the Potter's kiln—and as he was conformed to the image of Jesus, his life brought glory, honor, and praise to God.

*"I waited patiently for the Lord to help me,
and he turned to me and heard my cry.
He lifted me out of the pit of despair, out
of the mud and the mire. He set my feet on
solid ground and steadied me as I walked
along. He has given me a new song to sing,
a hymn of praise to our God."
—Psalm 40:1-3a, NLT*

My first profound encounter with God's personal dealings happened when I had been a believer less than two years. I had a zeal for the Lord, I read the Bible and prayed, and was always talking about Jesus whenever I had the opportunity. I wanted to be fully sold out for the Lord. I remember thinking, *I am going to be more zealous than Apostle Paul!* Of course looking back it was obvious that my zeal for the Lord was mixed together with a lot of soulish motivation including self-effort, self-confidence, and pride. My sincerity to serve the Lord was as pure as I could muster even as was Peter's sincerity when he boldly stated that he would never deny Christ. Many Christians looked at me and my fervent zeal and thought that I was really doing well. I couldn't understand why every Christian wasn't as sold out for the Lord as I was. I thought nothing would ever stop me from serving God fervently but then I didn't really understand my own heart.

I began to seek the baptism of the Holy Spirit soon after I accepted Christ; however, I did not receive it. At first this didn't bother me since I thought that soon I would receive this wonderful experience. But time stretched the days, weeks, and months into almost a year. When I went to church meetings where the Spirit of God was moving in a wonderful way, I felt nothing—I would be untouched. Other people would be baptized in the Holy Spirit and begin to speak in tongues, others would experience the tangible presence of God, while still others would receive visions and prophetic words. As more time passed, I grew frustrated. I began to murmur in my heart against God, *Why hasn't He baptized me in the Holy Spirit?* Instead of rejoicing at how God was blessing others, I resented the fact that I had not received the baptism. This negative attitude crept into my heart so gradually that I did not even recognize that it was there. However, my resolve to be baptized in the Holy Spirit remained strong and I continued to pray and seek the Lord on many different occasions.

Once a friend and I decided we would pray all night. He was already baptized in the Holy Spirit and he wanted to come alongside me as I sought the Lord. We were allowed access to the church and we began to pray. At first I was really excited and filled with expectation. But as the hours passed, I began to grow weary. We were still praying at 4 a.m. but it was apparent we were both very tired. I remember at one point my friend prayed, "Lord you know Howard desires to be baptized with Your Holy Spirit and You know how zealous he is and how he seeks you so diligently. If anyone *deserves* to be baptized in the Holy Spirit, Howard does." As he was praying those words I was in agreement. My self-effort and self-righteousness had so blinded me that I failed to see that the only reason we receive *anything* from the Lord is based solely on His grace and love through Jesus Christ. By the time night turned to dawn, I was exhausted and totally discouraged.

Slowly I became more and more disillusioned and bitter. My joy and zeal withered and discontentment, unthankfulness, and self-pity filled my heart. Then depression descended upon my soul. At first I didn't recognize it. It crept up like a mist—gradually. Finally I found myself in the grips of a full blown depression. Never in my life had I experienced such a deep dark pit. An oppressive presence continually engulfed me. Life was devoid of joy, pleasure, or hope. Sleep was the only relief I found, but each morning as I would begin to awaken—even before I was fully conscious—I would feel the black cloud of depression meet and envelop my being. This lasted for months. I do not know if it was two months or eight months. Just to face life day by day was a struggle. It seemed I had no hope for the future. Life was one black, bottomless, hopeless hole. A considerable change for someone who a short time before was going to be more zealous than Apostle Paul!

Throughout this time I continued to go to church and fellowship as best I could. I continued to read the Bible but the only book I could bear to read was Job. I didn't understand it very well, but I could certainly identify with the bitterness of soul that Job experienced. I cried out to God for help and like Job my cries were filled with anguish and complaining. I would cry out in prayer like Job, "Though He slay me, yet will I trust Him." I blamed God for my situation but at the same time I knew He was the only One I could turn to who could show me the way out. I thought this anguish would never end. I feared that my life would be one black pit until the day I died. Fear and depression became my constant companions.

Each time there was an altar call at a church service I would go up and repent and seek freedom from my misery but it felt like the heavens were brass. I would think, *Where is this God that saved me? Why doesn't He answer me? Why has He forsaken me?*

At the end of the summer of 1977, at the lowest point of my life, the church I attended had a youth summer camp for four days. My friend and I attended. There were morning and evening services with free time to enjoy the outdoors during the day. During every service while others praised the Lord, I would weep from sorrow and depression. Through my own selfishness I had unknowingly made wrong choices. Self-pity, unthankfulness, and bitterness had opened the door to the enemy who took me deep down the path of depression. Now I was a prisoner—hopelessly trapped and powerless to escape. It was a very fearful experience.

During every service I went up for the altar call and left in the same state that I came. I spoke to the visiting minister about my depression and anguish of soul. He looked at me and didn't seem to comprehend the depth of my agony. His response was simple: "What do you have to be depressed about? You're a healthy young man—just enjoy life."

On the third day of the camp meeting my friend and I decided to spend the afternoon in the cabin. I was miserable and he thought he would console me or at least keep me company. He was a faithful friend and had been with me through my whole journey into depression. As we sat in the cabin, I was on my bed and he sat on his, directly across from mine. There were no more words to speak—no more prayers to pray—nothing else to be done. Then one of us decided to read the Bible. We decided to read the book of Revelation, Chapters two and three. Seven churches are described there and each church received some type of rebuke; perhaps we could find a rebuke that would apply to me.

My friend began to read his Bible aloud while I followed in mine. We read the letter addressed to the church in Ephesus and how they were rebuked for losing their first love. After my friend read it we both said, "Maybe that is the problem." But somehow even though it was true that I had lost my first love, it didn't seem to be what the Holy Spirit was speaking. We read the letter to each church and each time we found no witness of the Spirit that it was for me—*and then it happened!*

My friend began to read from Revelation 3:7-13: *"And to the angel of the church in Philadelphia write, 'These things says He who is holy, He who is true, "He who has the key of David, He who opens and no one shuts, and shuts and no one opens": "I know your works. See, I have set before you an open door, and no one can shut it; for you have a little strength, have kept My word, and have not denied My name...Because you have kept My command to persevere, I also will keep you from the hour of trial which shall come upon the whole world, to test those who dwell on the earth. Behold, I am coming quickly! Hold fast what you have, that no one may take your crown. He who overcomes, I will make him a pillar in the temple of My God, and he shall go out no more. I will write on him the name of My God and the name of the city of My God, the New Jerusalem, which comes down out of heaven from My*

God. And I will write on him My new name. "He who has an ear, let him hear what the Spirit says to the churches." '

As he began to read the verse, *"I know your works. See, I have set before you an open door, and no one can shut it; for you have a little strength, have kept My word, and have not denied My name,"* all of a sudden I felt the presence of God as I had never before or since experienced. In one second of time I was overwhelmed by the peace and love of God. It was as if God was speaking those words directly to me. I was filled was such joy and a sense of God's love for me that tears instantly began to roll down my cheeks. I felt as if I was touching heaven. Every thought and feeling of depression, fear, and shame was instantly gone.

As I sat on my bed with tears running down my cheeks I thought to myself, *What is my friend going to think when he sees me crying?* Suddenly my friend stopped reading and looked up at me through the tears running down his face and he simply said, "This is for you, Howard." As I looked up at him I said "I know, I know." We had both experienced the exact same thing at the exact same moment. Then we dropped to our knees and began to worship the Lord while tears of joy flowed, and words of worship, praise, and thanksgiving poured out. I do not know how long it lasted. Perhaps minutes—perhaps a half hour—it was like worshipping before the Lord in heaven. Such joy and freedom! I began to understand the love and grace of God in a new way. What was astounding was that God had not rebuked me for all my failures, but extended His grace and mercy to me and said, "You have not denied My Name even though you have little strength and I have an open door which no man can shut." God's hand of mercy was extended to me.

From that moment the blackness of depression lifted and did not return. In the days that followed I had to resist the negative thought patterns I had developed over the preceding months, but the mountain of depression was broken. It took several weeks to change my negative thought patterns, but I did so by filling my mouth with praise and thanksgiving.

A friend later explained it to me this way. Oppression is like a fist being driven into soft clay. The oppression is removed when the fist is withdrawn, but the indentation of the fist is still evident, and the clay must be smoothed out. Every time I thought about that special visitation, it gave me strength to praise Him and change the habits and thought patterns that had developed. I now understood God loved me not because of who I am, but because of who He is. Through that experience, God did a deep work in my soul. It was a very painful experience but the benefits were glorious. I was able to experience God in a whole new dimension and also to have a greater understanding and compassion for others. God did a wonderful work in my heart.

Heavenly Father, I thank You for Your great and infinite patience with me even when I have been stubborn and self-willed. Forgive me for those times when I have not yielded to You and have been unwilling to accept the path on which You are leading me. Thank You for forgiving me and the wonderful way that You restore me through Your Son, Jesus Christ. Thank You Lord that You do not count my failures against me but that You always seek to make me whole. Help me to have a heart that embraces Your will. Cause my heart to be filled with thanksgiving and praise during unpleasant or even painful times. I know that as You lead me through difficult experiences, You are doing a wonderful work in my heart. Complete the good work You have begun in me so that my life will be able to fully glorify Your Name. Let there be nothing left in me that would bring shame or disgrace to my precious Savior, Jesus Christ. Amen.

OUR RELATIONSHIP WITH GOD'S PLAN
The Possessive Test

Our fifth essential relationship is with God's plan, and the test we must pass is the possessive test. It is interesting that we are at the fifth of seven steps and the clay has yet to be molded. We are often in a hurry to get into a visible ministry and we cannot wait to be greatly used by the grace of God, but there are four steps before we even get on the wheel, and go for a spin, so to speak. Throughout our Christian walk—from the day we received Christ and onward—we are to be a witness and a light to the world. But sometimes we are in a rush to be that vessel of glory, unwilling to follow God's timetable. Our very impatience is a sign of our immaturity.

In this fifth step, the ancient potter's considerable skill was called upon as he threw the clay with enough force and accuracy that it adhered to the exact center of the rotating wheel. It was imperative that the clay land in the exact center of the wheel. Unless the clay was perfectly centered, it would spin eccentrically and could not be molded. Similarly, we have to be Christ-centered when we are being shaped for His purposes. Colossians 1:18 says that Jesus must have preeminence over all things. Unless we are Christ-centered, we will be thrown off the wheel before we can be shaped into a vessel fit for God's use. All the fullness of God dwells in Christ, and in no one else. We cannot be trusted with God's plan until we have died to our own plans and ambitions. When we submit to God, He will engineer all our circumstances as a loving Father. Nothing happens by coincidence and we need to acknowledge Him in all things. We need to be able to say from our hearts as Jesus did, *"...I do not seek My own will but the will of the Father who sent Me."* (John 5:30b). Once we have surrendered our will to God's will and passed the possessive test, God can move His plan forward as He shapes us into the person He created us to be.

When the potter would place his hands on the clay to shape it, he positioned his thumbs down in order to raise the sides up. He never raised the sides up without pressing his thumbs down. So it is "thumbs down" on self, as we are hollowed out to be filled with His glory. We cannot be filled until we have first been emptied of our self-will. *The degree to which the clay is prepared determines the glory of the finished vessel.* As God shapes us, we may feel very empty sometimes, because it is His plan and not our plan. As the potter would shape the vessel, he frequently applied water to it with his hands to reduce friction and prevent the clay from tearing. The water on the potter's hands represents the grace of God. If we try to mold someone without grace, there will be a lot of friction, a lot of heat, and a lot of problems. In His grace, God uses the five-fold ministry, the five fingers of His hand, and the water of grace to eliminate friction as He shapes us.

The possessive test is passed by the acknowledgement that God is the Potter—we are not. We often want to tell the potter how we should be formed. Often our desires, our plans, where we want to be, and how we want to be used in ministry take priority over God's plans. If we take ownership of the plan, it becomes ours and ceases to be God's plan. We pass the possessive test by relinquishing our plans and surrendering to God's plan. It has to be *God's* plan.

One aspect of embracing God's plan and passing the possessive test is accepting not only how He will implement His plan, but also in accepting His timing. God placed a dream in Moses' heart to see Israel delivered from slavery and oppression but Moses in his rush to implement the plan killed an Egyptian. Moses spent forty years in the wilderness until, emptied of his plans and self-effort, he embraced God's methods and timing. Similarly Abraham had to learn to wait for God's timing to produce an heir; he fathered Ishmael out of his own timing and self-effort. Isaac was born according to God's timing and grace. Both men had the correct vision of God's plan but they needed to wait for God's perfect timing.

GOD'S PLAN FOR JOSEPH

How did Joseph relate to God's plan? Genesis 39:22-23 says, *"And the keeper of the prison committed to Joseph's hand all the prisoners who were in the prison; whatever they did there, it was his doing. The keeper of the prison did not look into anything that was under Joseph's authority, because the Lord was with him; and whatever he did, the Lord made it prosper."* Joseph was given authority over clothing, food, and every administrative matter necessary to run the prison. Because Joseph had proven himself trustworthy, the prison keeper did not even check on him. Even though he had authority over all prison matters, Joseph remained a prisoner and owned nothing. The provisions placed into his hands were not for Joseph's personal use, but to fill the needs of others. When we begin to understand that God has a ministry for each one of us, not to gratify us, but for the benefit of others, then we begin to understand the possessive test and what it means to be part of God's plan. Although Joseph personally owned nothing, he supplied everyone's needs, not from anything he owned, but from supplies given to him. This is a picture of true ministry. He learned what it meant to have authority over everything, but to personally possess nothing. Joseph could have favored himself, but he proved himself a faithful steward, realizing that even though he had been given authority, he possessed nothing; the provisions were for the benefit of the prisoners.

PAUL AND SILAS IN PRISON

Acts 16 describes a slave girl possessed with a spirit of divination. She brought her masters much money by fortune telling. Paul and Silas ministered to her and cast the evil spirit out of her. Her masters, seeing the loss of her moneymaking potential, brought Paul and Silas before the authorities, who beat them and threw them into the inner prison—the worst part of the prison. Paul and Silas were ministering, serving, and being faithful to God, and yet here they were in prison, physically abused and publicly humiliated. If Paul and Silas had failed the possessive test, God's plan would not have been fulfilled. But Paul and Silas had allowed God to mold them and they were emptied of their own agendas. Because they relinquished their ministry plan and accepted and embraced God's plan, they were able to flow in God's purposes, and rejoiced in God even while in jail. They accepted their imprisonment as part of God's plan and praised Him for it, offering *unconditional praise to God despite their adverse circumstances.* They submitted to God's plan with the right attitude, and God moved His plan forward through them to affect others. Paul and Silas prayed and sang praises to God in the midst of their prison. The word *praises* refers to "hallelujah praises." As the other prisoners heard them, they realized the two men were Christ-centered as they glorified God, in the midst of their difficulties.

THE EFFECT OF PAUL AND SILAS' SURRENDER TO GOD'S PLAN

Many people were affected because of Paul and Silas' acceptance of God's plan, as they passed the possessive test. After a while a great earthquake shook the prison and immediately the doors opened and everyone's bands were loosed. The word *earthquake* means "a shaking, a commotion, a tempest, an earthquake" and comes from a root word meaning "to shake up, to agitate." This word is also a metaphor for agitating the mind. Not only did an actual earthquake occur, but an earthquake took place within the minds of the prisoners. Acts 16:26 says that the foundation was shaken, and the word *foundation* can mean the foundation of a building, but it can also refer to a belief system. Sometimes we can be imprisoned by false systems of belief. The prisoners were in bondage—desperate—when suddenly their belief system was shaken as the doors swung open, and their shackles were loosened.

They were prisoners not just outwardly because of their chains and bars, but inwardly because of their false beliefs and attitudes, which held them in bondage as strongly as any iron chain. Those inward bonds controlled their thoughts, words, and actions, and their lives were imprisoned by them. As Paul and Silas praised God in the midst of adversity, the other prisoners were subjected to a new reality that they had never experienced before or even knew existed. Not only were their outward chains shaken, so were their inward ones. As God opened the door for them, they were affected both physically and spiritually—because Paul and Silas had surrendered to God's plan.

The second person to be affected was the keeper of the prisoners. Because he thought the prisoners had escaped, the guard thought to put himself to death than suffer death by torture at the hands of the Romans. *He didn't mind working for the Romans, but he wasn't too keen on their severance package!* The guard was also a prisoner, although he did not realize it. The guard was imprisoned by the Roman system. His soul had grown callous to the sufferings of others, and he was motivated by the selfish, self-seeking, and arrogant attitude embedded in him by the Roman Empire. His harsh and hardened heart was the chain that held him in bondage. When the guard saw the prison doors swing open, and death stared him in the face, Paul cried out in compassion to the guard not to harm himself. Through Paul's actions the guard was touched by the love of God. Paul saw the guard's need and responded with God's heart. Paul was not so overwhelmed with his own problems that he could not respond to the needs of others.

Paul centered his thoughts on Christ, and the Holy Spirit gave him a special sensitivity to the needs of those around him—even to those who were oppressing and persecuting him.

The guard responded by begging for a light, and he came into the cell and fell down before Paul and Silas. He had seen the light and asked the right question: *"Sirs, what must I do to be saved?"* (Acts 16:30). Consequently the guard and his entire household were saved. The guard ministered to Paul's wounds, and Paul baptized him and his family. Once again God's plan went forward because Paul passed the possessive test.

The authorities were the third group to be affected. Upon learning that Paul was a Roman citizen, they became frightened and asked Paul and Silas to leave the city. The actions of Paul and Silas, as well as the arrogant and unrighteous attitudes of the authorities, had been brought to light. The authorities were affected by the godly response of God's ministers, and pleaded with Paul in humility. This incident may have led to the believers in that city being given more freedom. Paul could have declared his citizenship earlier, but he did not try to escape; he waited for God's plan to be fulfilled and waited patiently through each step as he trusted God.

Yet a fourth group of people were affected as Paul and Silas continued on to Lydia's house where the miracles that God had performed were recounted to the believers. The church, as well as Paul and Silas, were comforted and encouraged, and a greater boldness was imparted to the believers to proclaim their faith. God did a work in each of the four groups, all because Paul and Silas surrendered to God's plan.

Today there are Christians in China and other countries who are suffering for the Gospel of Jesus Christ. To suggest that they are doing something wrong is untrue. If we wonder why we aren't being persecuted and suffering in a similar way, it is because God has a different plan for each of us. If we judge people according to our experience we will misunderstand them, because God is working out issues specific to each of our lives. One may appear to be suffering persecution for wanting to live a godly life in Christ Jesus, while another may appear to be having an easier time, but the truth is that God is leading each one into the unique plan He has for their lives.

Let us take the example of two vessels, a plate and a vase. One day the vase looks at the plate and says, "You know what? You're so shallow." And the plate looks back at the vase and says, "And you're so useless. At least I feed people, you just sit there looking pretty." We need to recognize that God is shaping all of us differently and uniquely so we can come together as the family of God, the Body of Christ. This is one excellent reason not to compare ourselves to others. We need to ask, "God, You placed me in this situation, how do You want me to respond? What do You want me to do? What is Your plan for me?"

Many people want to have a ministry, because it makes them feel important or meets an inner need. But this motivation is wrong and will always lead to problems. Gifted people, for example, sometimes possess a need to use their gifts because of their own self-centeredness or feelings of insecurity. That is *not* how we pass the possessive test. God has given us gifts and a ministry to meet the needs of others, not for self-gratification or to give us a sense of importance. We will be best able to serve God when both our actions and our motivations are conformed to His will and not our own.

In our relationship to God's plan, the test we must pass is the possessive test. The reason we must pass the possessive test is because it is God's plan, not ours, meant to bring about God's purposes for His glory and not our purposes for our glory. If we try to work out how to fulfill God's plan for our lives we will take into consideration many things that will either restrict or misdirect us. Some of these considerations might be our abilities, limitations, available resources, and the circumstances in which we find ourselves. These factors should not be ignored but if they become the criteria, we will have excluded

God. He is a God of surprises and loves to do things in sometimes unusual and unexpected ways. We must remember His plan is to be carried out in His way.

"I will instruct you and teach you in the way you should go; I will counsel you and watch over you."—Psalm 32:8, NIV

"God's way is perfect. All the Lord's promises prove true."—2 Samuel 22:31a, NLT

When I first became a Christian I had a desire to be a teacher of the Word of God and proclaim the truth of Christ. Not only was I totally unskilled at public speaking but at that time I was attending university to become a structural engineer. At one point I considered dropping out of university because I questioned the spiritual value of being an engineer. However, the Lord provided divine counsel that stopped me and showed me that He had a purpose in what I was studying.

I graduated from university, was married to a wonderful woman, and began working in my profession. Years went by and even though I was quite active in my local church, I felt that God was calling me into some type of ministry. From time to time I received prophetic words of confirmation. As the years passed, I sometimes felt I had missed out on God's purpose for my life. This led to feelings of frustration and helplessness about how to enter into that calling. I finally shelved all my concerns. I did not understand that during those years God was doing a work in my heart through each essential relationship such as obedience, separation, submission, and God's personal dealings with me to prepare me for His plan for my life.

It wasn't until seventeen years after I had first received Christ that God reawakened my hope to be used in ministry. During this time, I felt I had gained insights into God's Word and within my heart there was an explosion of revelation. However, I felt unable to effectively communicate these truths to others. Once the pastor of the church I attended asked me to share at a Sunday service. Since our church was small, I did not feel a great degree of pressure. However, when I tried to teach, the message was as dry as crackers.

How was I ever going to be a teacher of God's Word? One day a prophetic brother came to my home and said that the Lord had told him that it was time for me to start a Bible study in my home, which would grow quickly and would eventually become a church. I really wasn't very enthusiastic about the idea because I had not previously experienced success in that area. But as I sought counsel from those to whom I was spiritually accountable, we felt God saying the timing was right.

I prayed about how to implement this and decided on Monday nights. A few Christians were invited to come to the Bible study. Even though I was going through the motions I was quite pessimistic about what the results might be. I thought that either no one would show up or that those who did come would only come once and never return. But I resolved to obey the leading of the Holy Spirit even if it meant failure.

As I prayed about the first meeting the Lord quickened a number of things: first there would be a time of worship, then I would teach the Word, and then the Lord spoke to me clear as a bell —"After the teaching call the people up for prayer." I spent much time in prayer as I prepared the message based on some Biblical teachings I had studied.

Monday evening arrived and I was astonished that 25 people showed up. The Holy Spirit anointed the entire meeting. After the message, many came forward for prayer and the Lord, to my amazement, gave me a prophetic word for each person. The meeting lasted close to four hours.

After the meeting I thanked God for the blessing and the message. The message had been clear and powerful, but I thought, *That's all I have, I don't have anything to share for next week.* I thought the Lord had given me a very short ministry—*one day!*

The following week the Lord was faithful to quicken another message. Again there was a real anointing on the service and this time more people came—almost 35 people attended.

Week after week the meetings continued. Week after week the Lord gave me a fresh message. And week after week more people came. Soon we were averaging 60 to 80 people in our home. Sometimes it would top one hundred. I was grateful to my dear wife for supporting the endeavor even though our house was overrun with people. The neighbors thought we were having wild parties every Monday night.

Things were going well but I had no idea what we were to do next. How was a church going to come forth? After about three months, many were saying that we were ready to become a church. I sought counsel from our overseer but the word given to us continued to be, "Wait." I had learned about submission to authority—so I did what I was counseled to do—I waited. I encouraged everyone to continue to attend their local churches and faithfully serve there. I too continued to attend the local church to which I belonged. The pastor of the church we attended encouraged me regarding the Monday night meetings, which he sometimes attended. He also felt that eventually they could develop into a church, and being a truly openhearted pastor, he supported what God was doing. We continued to have Monday night meetings, months turned into years. What may have appeared to be lack of progress was really part of God's plan for shaping not only me, but those who would become part of the church and part of the team of elders. God matured me and those who attended the meetings. After three and a half years the Lord again spoke prophetically. It was now time to meet as a church. The pastor of the local church our family attended, when informed of the new church coming forth, had his entire congregation pray for my family and myself, and he released us with his blessing.

The Lord led us in putting together a team of elders and we began Sunday morning services. We met in a conference room on the ground floor of a high-rise apartment building. The room was 20 by 40 feet with a seven-foot high ceiling. Including children, about 65 people felt led to be part of this church. Every Sunday morning we met at this obscure location. We continued to hold the Monday night Bible study but the Sunday services were totally separate from the Bible study.

Over the next year the church grew only slightly even though the Monday night Bible study continued to flourish. Sometimes I would wonder, *What are you going to do next Lord? Are we just going to continue to be hidden in an apartment building meeting room?*

After meeting on Sundays for almost a year, the Lord put it on my heart that we needed to find a building we could rent for the exclusive use of the church. Again we prayed and sought the Lord. The Lord seemed to confirm this leading was from His Spirit.

Once as we were praying about a location, someone saw a vision of a very "churchy looking" building. When I heard the vision I immediately interpreted it metaphorically—meaning that God wanted to make us spiritually ornate. My concept of the type of building we were looking for was a very simple "non- religious" building without any of the trappings of religion. Once as we prayed someone had a vision of a church steeple. When I heard that I simply dismissed it. I thought, *What does a church steeple have to do with us finding a building for our church?*

The elders and I began to look for a suitable location. But none of the buildings we considered seemed to be the right one. After four months we were no closer to finding a location than when we began. One morning as I was praying I felt the Lord put it on my heart that we were not to look for a building any longer but simply seek Him in prayer. I shared this with my wife and her response was very reasonable, "It is important to pray but how are you going to find a building if you stop looking?" I knew that in the natural she was absolutely right but I felt that was the direction we were to go. I shared my conviction with the elders. They agreed. We decided to end each church service or prayer meeting by asking the Lord to show us the location He had already prepared for us. It was now nearly the end of December, 1999. As I was praying I asked the Lord to show us the location by March 1, 2000. I chose that date because it was the last day church information could be changed in the church directory for the city. Being an engineer I still wanted to be practical.

We shared with the congregation what we felt the Lord had shown us. We concluded every service with our petition for God to show us the location He had prepared for us. All of January went by and still nothing. The first weekend in February a friend of mine came from North Carolina to minister Sunday morning. After he concluded his message, we were about to close the service, and once again we petitioned the Lord for our new church location. As we were praying my friend spoke out a prophetic word, "Soon I will show you the location I have prepared for you. You have not yet seen it. It is much more than you have thought of or asked for." When I heard the prophecy the first thought that came to my mind was, *When is soon? Is that March first?* I didn't receive the prophetic word with a lot of enthusiasm. I took a wait and see approach.

After the service Don, who with his family had been coming to our church for about a year, approached me. He was in his forties and very reserved. He appeared somewhat perplexed. He began to tell me that he thought he might have seen the building. At first I though he had driven by a building that he thought would be suitable. But as he began to describe in detail the inside of the building, I realized that he had received a vision that morning as we were praying. Since he came from a denomination that does not believe in visions or the gifts of the Spirit, he didn't identify it as a vision—in fact he didn't know what to call it because he had never experienced anything like it before.

When he finished describing what he had seen, I told him I had no idea where such a building would be. I told him that if it were from the Lord then it would become apparent.

Three more weeks passed and one morning as I was praying I told the Lord, "Lord, this church was Your idea, not mine. You brought all these people together. You know we really need a building in which to meet. It is getting pretty close to March first and if You would show us the building by then I would really appreciate it." As I spoke to the Lord I felt a peace knowing it was in God's hands. I wish I could tell you that I prayed a prayer of faith and claimed that building and we had a breakthrough, but my prayer was much more conversational and subdued. I felt content to leave in it God's hands since it was His plan—I had no backup plan.

A few more days passed and then a member of the congregation called me and said that they saw a FOR SALE sign on an Anglican Church building in the downtown section of the city. As soon as he told me about it I immediately knew it was not for us. First, it was a very typical religious looking building. Second, we were not in a position to be purchasing a building for one or two million dollars. We were looking to rent and not buy. He gave me the church phone number from the sign. I wrote it down. The next day I went to work and half consciously left the number at home.

After lunch I decided to drive by the church building that was for sale. It was a very churchy looking building complete with a vaulted cathedral ceiling, stained glass windows, and a large steeple, which towered from one corner. When I saw the church building and the church steeple, the visions that we had previously heard described to us for some reason did not even enter my mind. All I saw was a churchy looking building that projected something that I did not want—probably with a big price tag to boot! Yet for some reason, I wrote down the telephone number as I drove by. When I returned to work I felt a nudging to make the call. But part of me was still resisting. It was not a spiritual concern—more like someone looking to buy a used car who would feel foolish inquiring about a Porsche.

I finally decided to call. The church secretary answered the phone. I inquired if the building was still for sale. She told me that it was. When I asked the price she told me they were asking $285,000. That was when my interest really piqued because I love a bargain! You couldn't even buy the land to build a church for that amount. I asked if I could see it. A few minutes later a church trustee phoned and we arranged a meeting. That afternoon as I came to see the building, I noticed a prostitute sitting on the steps of the church trying to solicit business. Also in front of the church drug deals were being conducted. I thought to myself, *This is great! We won't even have to bus these people in—they're already here. It will be like fishing in a stocked pond.*

The main church building was built in 1895. The vaulted ceiling was beautifully finished in wood and towered almost 30 feet—quite a contrast to the seven-foot high ceiling where we were meeting. There were Sunday school rooms downstairs. In the back was a gymnasium with a full size stage. The gym had been built in 1954. The building was in excellent condition. That evening the elders saw the building and we all felt that this was perhaps the answer to our prayers but we were still unsure. The next morning, a Friday, we contacted the entire congregation and asked them to pray and fast on Saturday regarding this building and asked that if the Lord showed them something to phone us.

That morning Don, who had seen a vision of the inside of a building a few weeks before, decided to drive by the church building. As he arrived the church secretary was leaving and she invited him to see inside the building. She showed him the sanctuary, then the Sunday school rooms downstairs, and then she took him into the gym. When he entered the gym he almost fell over. It was exactly what he had seen in detail in the vision. He was overwhelmed. When he returned home he called me and told me what he had seen. Then I recalled the details he had described to me a few weeks before when he first received the vision. It finally clicked in my mind as well. The gymnasium, the stage, the orientation of the stairs, and the type of windows were all just as he had described them to me a few weeks before. I was excited and Don was filled with amazement at what he had seen. Even more interesting was that the church building had only been put up for sale three days before we found it, but he had received the vision almost three weeks before. God is always the best real estate agent—He knows the deals before they even come on the market.

The next day as each person in the congregation spent time in fasting and prayer they all felt that this was from the Lord and they were all in agreement. God was going to take a church comprised of middle and working class people, and plant us right in the middle of the most crime-ridden street in the city.

But even with all of this confirmation, we as a leadership team sought more confirmation. The Word of God says to let every word be confirmed by two or three witnesses. This was a very important decision and if God was not in it then we would be swallowed up by the crime, drug abuse, and prostitution that surrounded the church building and the area. We sought counsel and prayer with those who provided oversight for the church. Through all these people the Lord continued to confirm that this really was from Him and that the time was right to purchase the building.

We purchased the building and took possession of it July first of that year. We actually found the building a couple of days before the March first deadline, and were able to have our address changed in the city church directory.

When we finally took possession of the church, I stood at the pulpit inside the empty church building. I looked out at the cathedral ceiling, the stained glass windows, the ornate church décor and re-membering the prostitutes and the drugs dealers working outside the doors of the church, I said out loud laughingly, "What's a good Jewish boy like you doing in a place like this!?" Truly God's plans and ways are much different than we could ever imagine.

Despite my reluctance to move into a churchy looking building, the Lord used its traditional appearance to give us instant acceptance in the neighborhood—we looked the way they expected a church to look. Because we are not affiliated with a particular denomination, the church's appearance gave the neighbors a comfort level with the church they might not have had if we had relocated in a "store-front" building—where they might have been suspicious, or even thought of us as a cult. As Christians, we know that the church building does not define a church. But to people who have never been exposed to the Gospel, or who have had limited exposure, the appearance of our building represented what they expected a church to look like. Because we are located in a church that *looks* like a church, people from the neighborhood have come to us when they have found themselves in a crisis, and have found salvation through Jesus Christ. God used the traditional appearance of this building to give us legitimacy in the neighborhood we might not have otherwise enjoyed.

When we moved in, the Lord had one more revelation to surprise us and to confirm this was truly His leading. One Ukrainian Christian brother whose daughters came to our church came by to drop off one of his daughters to help clean the day we took possession of the church. He was attending a Ukrainian Pentecostal church at the time. As he stepped into the sanctuary he looked around and said, "I can't believe this!" His daughter asked him what was wrong. He said that eleven years before when they left Ukraine as refugees they had first spent a year and a half in Austria waiting to come to Canada. One day while praying he asked the Lord what church He wanted him to attend. The Lord gave him a vision of the inside of a church building filled with people. For the past eleven years every time he went inside a church he was always looking for the one he had seen in the vision. This was the church he had seen eleven years before in his vision.

Before we had even found the building, the Lord had given four people visions of the building and one person a dream. All these confirmations from the Lord were an encouragement but also something we needed to hold on to when things were not going smoothly. God's plans are glorious but they are not always easy. We need to be totally dependant upon the leading of the Holy Spirit so we move in His plan and not our own. We need to let go of the steering wheel so God can direct us and we can pass the possessive test.

One thing that is important is that we not try to reproduce what God has done elsewhere, but that we seek His plan for us individually. Our God and Father is infinitely creative and leads each one of us in very unique and personal ways. The Lord may lead another church to find a building using a real estate agent or other means. The method is not important—what is important is that we seek and submit to the leading of the Holy Spirit.

Heavenly Father, I am awed at the perfection and beauty of Your plan and how You so wonderfully weave everything together for good when I am loving and trusting You. Forgive me for those times that I have questioned Your plan and allowed worry and doubt to fill my heart. Forgive me for those times when I have not trusted Your plan but tried to take things into my own hands. Remind me to reflect on the ways You have faithfully led me and helped me to draw faith and encouragement through these meditations. I look forward to those things that lay ahead. Your ways are perfect and I praise You for the wonderful surprises You bring to me as I trust in You. Amen.

OUR RELATIONSHIP WITH GOD HIMSELF
The Priority Test

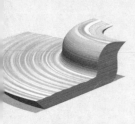

The sixth essential relationship—with God himself—can be divided further into three distinct types of relationship—with God the Father, God the Son and God the Holy Spirit. The priority test demands that we have a personal relationship with God Himself. This is the place where we really get to know God, but to know Him, we have to set our priorities in the right order. Christ is our friend—but the question is this: *"Are we His friend?"* (John 15:12-15). Are we willing to lay down our life for Jesus? God has to be first—ahead of ministry and anything else. He alone is first and everything else is secondary.

Since God is a triune being, we have a tripartite relationship with Him. These three essential relationships are illustrated in Philippians 3:3. *"For we are the circumcision, who worship God in the Spirit, rejoice in Christ Jesus, and have no confidence in the flesh..."*

OUR RELATIONSHIP WITH GOD THE FATHER – THE REST TEST

The first relationship is our relationship with God the Father and the accompanying test is the rest test. After the clay was shaped by the potter on the wheel, it would be too soft and delicate to be handled, and very susceptible to damage. So the potter would very carefully place the vessel on a shelf where it remained until it became "leather hard," dry to the consistency of leather. It had to rest there; if it was touched before it dried, it became distorted. If it were fired while the clay remained damp, the vessel would self-destruct in the kiln, blown apart from the steam generated by the oven's heat. Resting was essential. This is learning to worship God in spirit and resting in the Father's presence.

Potters refer to pots at this stage of development as green ware. We may feel that because we now have the *form* of a vessel, we are ready to minister to others, but we may still be pretty "green." First Timothy 5:22 admonishes: *"Do not lay hands on anyone hastily..."* The context of this Scripture refers to the installation of elders into positions of authority. The warning speaks about the apostolic responsibility of ensuring that the person being installed has the maturity, experience, and purity necessary for the position.

One of the qualifications listed by Apostle Paul for an elder is that he *"not be a novice."* (1 Timothy 3:6). The Greek word for *novice* means "newly planted." In other words, he is not to be "green," but a man of maturity and experience. It is very interesting that Paul identifies the danger of placing a novice into ministry, *"lest* [he be] *puffed up with pride."* The vessel appears ready to serve from the outside, but the moisture within it will cause it to blow apart (be puffed up with pride) when it comes into contact with the fire of the kiln (God's glory). The qualified man knows his finite limitations as well as God's infinite *lack* of limitations. We must know in the very depth of our being that God uses us only because of His grace, mercy, and love—not because we have any special qualities of ourselves—so when God uses us, we will not be tempted to touch His glory.

Some young Christians feel they can do nothing until they come to spiritual maturity while other young Christians feel that they are equipped to instruct and teach on everything to everybody. We need to know the depth of our experience with God and our own limitations. Young Christians should be encouraged to step out in faith in those areas where they have experienced God. We need to minister in reality and not in theory. If we minister solely out of theory, we are still "green." What we are teaching may be correct, but it is not supported by spiritual maturity or personal experience.

First Thessalonians 5:16-18 says, *"Rejoice always, pray without ceasing, in everything give thanks; for this is the will of God in Christ Jesus for you."* When Paul spoke those words, he was not ministering out of theory, but personal experience. He knew God's faithfulness as he was fired in the crucible of a Roman prison. His enemies were many and mighty—yet Paul was found faithful to rest in God for His timing and plan to go forward. Through his trials, Paul was conformed into the image of the Lord Jesus, and God's will for his life bore abundant fruit. Apart from his ministry and oversight to the churches, much of the New Testament was written while he served time in Roman prisons.

When we are in a rush to do things for God without an establishing an intimate relationship of waiting on Him, we too will become distorted. There are many warped Christians in this world because they have not learned to rest in the presence of the Father, and have failed the rest test. God wants us to be "Godaholics," not workaholics, not ministry driven, or driven by anything else, but to sit quietly in the presence of God and allow consistency to develop in our spiritual walk so that we will be balanced and not distorted.

Joseph had to learn to wait on God and rest in His presence, recognizing God's sovereignty and that God, not Joseph, was in control. That is how we worship in Spirit. Joseph allowed God to do what would bring Him the most glory.

OUR RELATIONSHIP WITH GOD THE SON— THE FAITHFULNESS TO THE VISION TEST

Our second relationship is with the Son and we are tested in our faithfulness to the vision. After the green clay had dried to the consistency of leather, it would be removed from the shelf, and placed upside down on the wheel. First the potter wrote his initials on the bottom of the pot, signifying that it was his work. Once again he spun the pot on the wheel, filling in any indentations and carefully shaving off any surplus clay. In this step God removes any eccentricities in our character so the focus will not be on us but on the Lord Jesus. It is noteworthy that this whole process occurred while the vessel was upside down.

In our relationship with the Son, there will be times in our lives when everything feels upside down, when nothing in our lives is going as we think it should. We may ask, "God, what are You doing? Nothing's making sense." The test we need to pass in our relationship with the Son of God is the faithfulness to the vision test, to keep our eyes on the Lord Jesus.

When life seems confusing and nothing seems to make sense—when our world seems turned upside down—that's when we need to pass the priority test. We need not become discouraged, but instead to hold fast to the vision, which is the person of Jesus Himself. Our priority must be Jesus Christ. During times of apparent turmoil we must fix our eyes on Jesus, the author and finisher of our faith (Hebrews 12:2), who did not allow the shame or pain of the cross to shift His focus from the Father's purpose for His life. We need to learn to rejoice in Jesus. He must be the purpose and focus of our joy so that even in the midst of circumstances filled with turmoil, we remain unshaken.

In Joseph's life we see that he passed this test, that even while in prison his faith did not fail. Through that experience Joseph learned not to second-guess God but to hold on to the word given to him. Joseph kept his vision on God who remained his only hope as every other possibility had been removed.

OUR RELATIONSHIP WITH GOD THE HOLY SPIRIT – THE GRACE TEST

Our third relationship is with the Holy Spirit and the accompanying test is the grace test. After the vessel became uniform in texture and form, the potter applied colored powder as ornamentation. This ornamentation was not achieved using the Egyptian method, where the glaze was only applied to the surface. In the hands of the Israelite potter, the colored powder was applied to the clay so that it slightly penetrated the surface; the ornamentation actually became part of the clay, indicating a deeper work. In a similar fashion when the Holy Spirit begins to decorate us with His gifts, they become part of our nature. When Eliezer, Abraham's chief servant—and a prefigure of the Holy Spirit—searched for a bride for Isaac, he found Rebekah. When he found her, he put gold and silver jewelry on her and made her ornate. In a similar manner, the Holy Spirit wants to beautify us as part of our preparation for the Lord Jesus.

After the clay vessel was decorated it would receive its initial firing. This firing did not last for a prolonged period of time; its purpose was simply to set the colored embellishment into the vessel. We are baptized in the Holy Spirit and fire. After the initial firing the vessel would be removed from the kiln and burnished. Small fragments of broken pottery were rubbed against the pot to polish it, intensifying its color, and revealing its beauty. Similarly, God uses broken vessels to burnish us—to bring out the beauty of Jesus in us. We see people with problems and think, *Oh, that person's trouble,* and want to have nothing to do with them. However, in reality, God has placed those very people in our lives to "rub us the wrong way" and create friction so we can learn to rely on the Holy Spirit and respond in grace. The broken pottery is a picture of the broken people that God uses to burnish us, to bring out the beauty of Christ within us. We must learn to have no confidence in the flesh but to depend totally on the Holy Spirit at all times.

JOSEPH'S RELATIONSHIP WITH GOD HIMSELF

Joseph's incarceration in the prison proved to be an important time in his spiritual growth. In that setting, God dealt with three specific areas in Joseph's relationship with God, namely: "God's Personal Dealings," his "Relationship to God's Plan," and his "Relationship With God Himself." In Joseph's life, this sixth essential relationship (with God Himself) was developed in him while he remained confined to prison. Joseph came to the realization that only by God's grace and by His Spirit, could the work be completed in him. During his last two years in prison, Joseph passed the priority test. He came to a place of complete reliance on God.

God often uses wilderness experiences in the lives of godly men and women to shape them into vessels for His glory. For example, during the forty years that Moses tended sheep, God transformed his character from one of being self-reliant and impulsive, to one of humility and sensitivity to the needs of His own sheep, the children of Israel. During his time in seclusion, God shaped Moses to be the vessel who would fulfill His plan to deliver the Israelites from Egypt.

What do we see when we observe Joseph's relationship with God? Genesis 40:1-4 says, *"It came to pass after these things that the butler and the baker of the king of Egypt offended their lord, the king of Egypt. And Pharaoh was angry with his two officers, the chief butler and the chief baker. So he put them in custody in the house of the captain of the guard, in the prison, the place where Joseph was confined. And the captain of the guard charged Joseph with them, and he served them; so they were in custody for a while."*

In Genesis 40:3, the phrase *captain of the guard* means "a guardsman, a body guard," but it can also mean "executioner." In other words the captain of the guard could cause someone to die. The specific Hebrew word for *prison* is *cohar*, which literally means "house of roundness, roundhouse, prison." It is used only eight times in the Bible and all in references to the prison where Joseph was confined. It has spiritual significance because it implies there were no corners and no place for Joseph to hide. Every issue in his heart was exposed in order to be resolved. God used this special type of prison to perform a special type of work. The word *custody* means "to confine, to post guard," but it can also mean "to observe, to give heed." When verse three mentions that Joseph was confined, the word *confined* means "to be tied" but it can also mean "to begin the battle, make the attack." By incorporating the Hebrew meanings of the words, this verse could be rephrased this way: "So he put the butler and the baker into a place where they could be observed, in the house of the chief executioner, in the house of roundness where there are no corners to hide in or conceal anything, the place where Joseph was embattled."

I believe God spoke to Joseph prophetically through these two men about the battle that raged in his soul between his spirit and flesh. God placed Joseph in a place where nothing could be hidden, where the sinful nature had to be executed, and where the spirit of life could be liberated. Joseph needed to deal with the things in his soul that kept him in prison. Many Christians appear outwardly to be free, but they have areas of bondage in their souls from the past. We need to do battle to be set free from our shackles. Joseph battled the order of his priorities, a battle we all face, to follow after the spirit and not the flesh.

Joseph was instructed to serve the butler and baker, and he came to know them personally during their confinement. God prepared Joseph to receive the Word of the Lord through their dreams, not only for their own lives, but for Joseph's life as well. *"Then the butler and the baker of the king of Egypt, who were confined in the prison, had a dream, both of them, each man's dream in one night and each man's dream with its own interpretation."* (Genesis 40:5). One day they looked sad and when Joseph asked why, they explained that they each had a dream and wanted an interpretation. The butler and the baker's dreams spoke prophetically to Joseph about the intense battle within his soul that prevented him from passing the priority test.

THE BUTLER'S DREAM

The butler's dream represented life in the spirit. For a born-again New Testament believer, the butler represents our reborn spirit. The word *butler* in Hebrew means "to irrigate, to water, give drink to," and is a beautiful picture of the Holy Spirit. John 7:38 tells us that out of our hearts will flow rivers of living water. It is our inner spirit that brings forth life and fills our soul with all the things of God. So the butler's dream is a prophetic picture of our spirit.

"Then the chief butler told his dream to Joseph, and said to him, 'Behold, in my dream a vine was before me, and in the vine were three branches; it was as though it budded, its blossoms shot forth, and its clusters brought forth ripe grapes. Then Pharaoh's cup was in my hand; and I took the grapes and pressed them into Pharaoh's cup, and placed the cup in Pharaoh's hand.' And Joseph said to him, 'This is the interpretation of it: The three branches are three days. Now within three days Pharaoh will lift up your head and restore you to your place, and you will put Pharaoh's cup in his hand according to the former manner, when you were his butler.'" (Genesis 40:9-13). God was promising to restore the spirit into a rightful place of authority in Joseph's life.

In his dream the butler saw three branches come forth. The Bible says that Jesus is the vine and we are the branches. The branch buds, blossoms, and brings forth great fruit, which is a picture of the spirit. The word *vine* can mean "a vine of prosperity." God wants us to make it a priority to dwell in our spirit, so that we may prosper in all the good things of God, and be filled with the love, joy, and peace of God.

The butler then took the grapes and filled Pharaoh's cup with the fruit of the vine, that is, with fruitfulness. The cup represents our soul. God wants to fill our soul with all the goodness of God. But our spirit must take hold of our soul in order that it may be filled. Being led by the spirit requires our soul to yield to the spirit's leading until the priorities of spirit and soul become one. Not until the grapes are pressed by trials is the juice brought forth. Romans 8:17b-18 says, *"...if indeed we suffer* (that is the squeezing) *with Him, that we may also be glorified* (that is the filling) *together. For I consider that the sufferings of this present time are not worthy to be compared with the glory which shall be revealed in us."* God places pressure on our souls to bring forth His glory. We have to endure the squeezing in order to receive the filling; we endure the suffering to be filled with His glory.

The grapes in the butler's vision also represent the fruit of the Spirit in our lives. The fruit of the Spirit is the manifestation of the life of Christ within our soul. The fruit of the Spirit is singular. Although Galatians 5:22-23 describes nine characteristics, all are the fruit of love, unable to be subdivided. For example, we will only have patience if we have love. In contrast the gifts of the Spirit operate individually within us to minister to the body of Christ, and are a manifestation of the Holy Spirit ministering to others. As the life of Christ increases in our vessel more of the fruit of the Spirit is manifest. When we have the *fruit* of the Spirit in our lives, the *gifts* of the Spirit operate beautifully, in love, as described in 1 Corinthians, Chapter 13. God desires to conform us into the image of Jesus, and what does Jesus look like? The fruit of the Spirit is a description of our Savior!

THE BAKER'S DREAM

The baker represents our old sinful nature. When the interpretation of the butler's dream proved favorable, the baker decided to tell Joseph his dream. The old self-life is not interested in the truth but only in words that tickle the ears. The old man in us does not want correction, only affirmation. *"When the chief baker saw that the interpretation was good, he said to Joseph, 'I also was in my dream, and there were three white baskets on my head. In the uppermost basket were all kinds of baked goods for Pharaoh, and the birds ate them out of the basket on my head.' So Joseph answered and said, 'This is the interpretation of it: The three baskets are three days. Within three days Pharaoh will lift off your head from you and hang you on a tree; and the birds will eat your flesh from you.'"* (Genesis 40:16-19).

In contrast to the butler who was to be restored to his position of authority, the baker was to lose his head and be hung on a tree. The old nature must no longer hold a position of influence over us (lose its head); it has been crucified (hung on a tree) with Christ. (Romans 6:6). Our priorities are correctly aligned when, *"Likewise you also, reckon yourselves to be dead indeed to sin, but alive to God in Christ Jesus our Lord."* (Romans 6:11). The phrase *baked goods* refers to a variety of leavened breads, which speaks of man's corrupt thoughts. Jesus alone is the bread of life and our own self-effort can never sustain us. The word *goods* means "works, achievements," and refers to our self-life.

The baked goods in the baker's dream are in vivid contrast to the vine in the butler's dream because much labor was required to produce them, whereas the vine simply grew up and the butler had only to crush the fruit. Compare the two dreams: the butler's dream was about an empty vessel that needed to be filled, while the baker's dream was about a full vessel that needed to be emptied. The baker, representing the old sinful nature, had three baskets on his head. The Hebrew word for *basket* comes from the Hebrew root word meaning "to lift up, exalt." The old nature exalts the mind so that the enemy can fill us with thoughts and doubts that are contrary to God's Word and His ways. Second Corinthians 10:4-5 speaks about those wrong ways of thinking as strongholds that must be pulled down. Galatians 5:16-17 says, *"I say then: Walk in the Spirit, and you shall not fulfill the lust of the flesh. For the flesh lusts against the Spirit, and the Spirit against the flesh; and these are contrary to one another, so that you do not do the things that you wish."* The Spirit desires that we would be filled with all the goodness of God but the flesh craves and desires to draw us into sin. Both desire to have dominion, but only one can have priority in our lives.

The word *chief* used to describe both the butler and baker actually means "a ruler." They were called the ruling butler and the ruling baker. As carnal Christians, we experience an ongoing conflict within us; both the old man with his old ways, and the new man with his new ways, are trying to rule us. Romans 7:25 says, *"I thank God—through Jesus Christ our Lord! So then, with the mind I myself serve the law of God, but with the flesh the law of sin."* Part of us wants to serve God, while another part draws us away from God. Romans, Chapter 8, further expands on this battle between our old self-life and the life of Christ within our spirit. Both parts are chiefs who want to rule over us, but only one of them can be in charge.

A similar picture of the spirit in conflict with the flesh is seen in Abraham's two sons. Galatians 4:22-24 says, *"For it is written that Abraham had two sons: the one by a bondwoman, the other by a freewoman. But he who was of the bondwoman was born according to the flesh, and he of the freewoman through promise, which things are symbolic. For these are the two covenants: the one from Mount Sinai which gives birth to bondage, which is Hagar."* The story of Isaac and Ishmael is an allegory for the two covenants. Ishmael represented the old covenant of the law because he was under bondage being born to the slave woman. Isaac was the son born through God's promise. Their story helps us to understand the old and the new covenants, the law and grace.

In the butler and the baker we also see the bread and the wine as reminders of communion. The blood of Jesus speaks about His sacrifice and the giving of His life, while the bread represents His flesh being broken for us, and His death. The baker represents the old man whose authority over our lives needs to be crucified. The Scripture says we were crucified with Christ, that we died with Christ, and that our old nature is crucified. We need to make that a reality in our lives on a daily basis by acting in faith and reckoning our old nature crucified with Christ.

At the time of his encounter with the baker and the butler, Joseph was in the sixth stage of development in his relationship with God Himself. Not only were the two dreams personally prophetic for the butler and the baker—the dreams were also a prophetic word for Joseph, although the two servants did not realize it. Genesis 40:13-18 says that on the third day the butler would be restored, and the baker would be crucified—hung on a tree. Although Joseph asked the butler not to forget him, the butler did forget him. On the third day Pharaoh had a birthday party, and he decided to hang the baker and restore the butler to a position of authority, but the butler forgot Joseph. Even though man had forgotten Joseph, God had not!

The precision regarding the prophetic timing laid out in the butler's dream applied to both himself and to Joseph with remarkable accuracy. Sometimes in Scripture we see the principle of a day representing a year. For example, Ezekiel 4:6b says, *"I have laid on you a day for each year."* The fulfillment of the dream took place on the third *day* for the butler, but the fulfillment of his dream took place in the third *year* in Joseph's life in prison. *"Then it came to pass, at the end of two full years, that Pharaoh had a dream; and behold, he stood by the river."* (Genesis 41:1). Two full years had passed and Joseph was into his third year in prison when Pharaoh himself had a dream. On the third *day* the butler was restored and the baker hanged; in the third *year* Pharaoh had a dream and Joseph was removed from prison. In the intervening two years, God had shown Joseph the two natures in his soul. By the third year the work was complete and Joseph had set the priorities in his life in divine order.

The butler and the baker are also a picture of the two covenants, of grace and of the law. The principles of the law were applied to the baker and the principles of grace to the butler. The law brings judgment, but through Christ's suffering and death, our old sinful nature has been judged because we have been crucified with Christ. In the butler's life, we see God's grace in operation. Just as the butler was released from his prison to serve Pharaoh, through our reborn spirit and by the grace of God, we have been released from the bondage of sin by our resurrected Savior to serve God.

When Joseph interpreted the butler's dream, he added, *"But remember me when it is well with you, and please show kindness to me; make mention of me to Pharaoh, and get me out of this house."* (Genesis 40:14). Joseph knew that the baker was a dead end, that self-effort could never release him from prison. Our flesh will never free us of our predicaments, or solve our problems. It is always the spirit and not our flesh that releases us from prison. So Joseph appealed to the butler, a picture of the spirit, to release him.

Genesis 41:14 refers to a *dungeon* which means "a pit" but the word can also mean "a well or cistern" and comes from the root word "to make clean, to explain, to prove." In the "dungeon" where God sometimes confines us, His Word is available to water and sustain us, and to bring revelation and clarification. The dungeon can be a difficult place, and at first we may resist turning to His Word, but when we do we will find a fresh stream flowing in what was a dry pit. God wants to make His purposes clear so we will understand. The word *dungeon* was first used in Joseph's story when his brothers threw him into the pit in Genesis 37:24. The words *pit* and *dungeon* are the same Hebrew word. Joseph never really came out of the pit, he just moved from one pit to another, as God continued to deal with him. God showed Joseph that the pit was not a place of destruction, but one where he would find the clarification and self-understanding that would ultimately bring his freedom.

In this sixth relationship, God wants to correctly align our priorities so that we may say, as the Apostle Paul said in his letter to the Philippians: *"Not that I speak in regard to need, for I have learned in whatever state I am, to be content: I know how to be abased, and I know how to abound. Everywhere and in all things I have learned both to be full and to be hungry, both to abound and to suffer need. I can do all things through Christ who strengthens me."* (Philippians 4:11-13). Unless our priorities are correct, we will only be happy when we abound. But even if we abound, our happiness will be short-lived because selfishness can never be satisfied. God wants us to be content in whatever situation He puts us, not because the situation is good or bad, but because God is inherently good and is doing a beautiful work in our lives. God is our El Shaddai, the all sufficient One.

The word *content* means "sufficient for one's self, strong enough," but it also means "to be independent of external circumstances." The Greek word for *learn* means "to be initiated into the mystery." Paul was initiated into the mystery of how to be content in every situation. To learn a mystery is not something we study in a classroom or learn in casual conversation—it occurs by communion—in secret. While in that dark place, Joseph learned from the Spirit to order his priorities according to God's ways. In the depths of his prison, he learned the mystery—to be content with God's provision and with the sweetness of his fellowship with the Lord. When Joseph finally stood before Pharaoh, Pharaoh did not see a man who felt the best years of his life had been stolen—or a man bitter or disappointed—but one who was content in God's leading, and confident in God's provision. We need to be independent of external circumstances to move on with God. We need to fully realize that God is sovereign; that is the key to being set free from prison and bondage, to have a relationship with God, and to know Him fully.

Jonathan Edwards, whose preaching in the American colonies brought about the "Great Awakening" in 1734-35, was persecuted and treated with hostility. Yet it was said of him, "...but he appeared like a man of God, whose happiness was out of the reach of his enemies." Like Paul and Joseph before him, his happiness was independent of external circumstances.

While Joseph remained in prison, he passed the three tests corresponding to the sixth essential relationship: first he passed the 'rest test' by learning to wait on the Father for His timing. He passed the faithfulness to the vision test by never giving up on the truth of God's Word to him. Joseph must have thought his interpretation of the two dreams would secure his ticket out of prison. But when the butler was released, he apparently forgot all about Joseph. Joseph must have thought, *I don't understand this; it doesn't make any sense. I thought I was doing things right, but everything is still upside down. God gave me the dreams and the interpretation and I thought it obvious that was to be my way of leav-*

ing this prison. But now I haven't even heard from the butler. However, Joseph remained faithful to the vision God had given him. He kept his eyes on the Lord and held fast to God's calling regardless of how his circumstances appeared. He did not allow despair or depression to settle in his heart but held on to the promises of God for his life.

Finally Joseph passed the third test, 'the grace test,' by developing such an intimate relationship with the Holy Spirit, that when God spoke to him, he could speak God's word to Pharaoh without any hesitation. Only if we understand how completely Joseph passed the overall priority test, can we fully appreciate Joseph's conduct as he stood before Pharaoh. Joseph never mentioned any of the injustices he had endured, nor did he plead not to be sent back to prison. He stood before Pharaoh resolute—with one purpose—to deliver the Word of the Lord to Pharaoh. Contrast his behavior here with his response two short years before, when the primary concern he expressed to the butler was being released from prison.

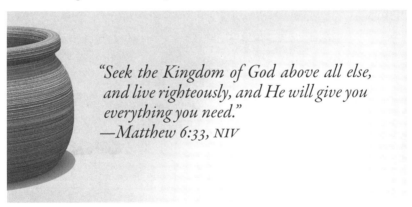

"Seek the Kingdom of God above all else, and live righteously, and He will give you everything you need."
—Matthew 6:33, NIV

The sixth essential relationship deals with our relationship with God Himself and the overall test we must pass is the priority test. God must come first—before everything else. Because God is a triune being there are three aspects to this test.

In our relationship with God the Father, the test we must pass is the rest test. This relates to the overall priority test in that if our priorities are improperly aligned our time spent in the presence of the Lord can become rushed and we will be unable to clearly hear from God. One of the things that God uses to test us in this area is our success. The more success we have the greater the lure for us to get our priorities out of order.

One example of a time when I needed correction in this area occurred about two years after we began the Monday night Bible study. The Bible study was bursting at the seams. Often people who came to the Bible study would tell me that every Monday morning when they woke up they would be really excited because they knew that night they could come to the Bible study. During that time I spent a few hours each day in personal prayer and studying God's Word. Many evenings I visited with people and shared the Word or prayed with them. People were really being blessed and I thought things couldn't be better. I was filled with excitement and joy as I served the Lord.

A Christian brother from Indiana came to visit us for a few days, and when he saw how the Monday night meetings were going, he was really encouraged by what God was doing. During the last day of his visit he shared a dream with me that he had the previous night. In the dream he saw me speeding down a highway. On the left side of the highway were large neon signs. Some said BUSINESS, others said NEEDS, while others said MINISTRY. They were attractive signs, which easily caught my attention. There were more signs on the opposite side of the road. They were much smaller and without the fancy graphics and bright lights. These signs were caution signs. Some read WATCH FOR FALLING ROCKS. One read BRIDGE OUT, and beside that sign was the name of my youngest son Jonathan, who was four years old at that time. Another sign read SPEED TRAP and beside it the name of my second son Danny who was twelve. Another sign read SLOW ZONE and beside it was name of my oldest son Jacob, then fourteen. Still another read CURVE AHEAD and my wife's name, Lena, was written beside that sign—*and I am not going to tell you how old she was!*

As he shared the dream with me the interpretation became apparent. I experienced a mixture of emotions. I was thankful that the Lord had given this brother the dream and that he loved me enough and had the courage to share his dream with me. I felt a sense of failure and shame for neglecting my family without recognizing it. I wasn't as spiritually mature and sensitive to the Holy Spirit as I had thought. Although at that time there did not appear to be any particular stresses in my family or my marriage, I realized that I had neglected ministering to the needs of my wife and children. My wife had tolerated my lack of sensitivity as I had been caught up with work during the day and ministry during the evenings. If I had continued on that path, I would have caused great damage to my relationship with my wife and would have only distant and strained relationships with my children.

My initial response was humiliation. If humiliation is the fertilizer for humility, I felt well fertilized that morning! By God's grace I repented. Even though I spent time in prayer every day with the Lord, I had not passed the rest test because my focus was more on what God was doing than on God Himself. As I turned to the Father, He restored my sensitivity to the needs of my wife and children. God has blessed me over the years with a wonderful marriage and children that love the Lord. My wife, Lena, has not only been supportive, but has been a true partner in ministry. But if I had continued on the path I was following, my children might have grown up resenting the church because it would have stolen time and attention that belonged to them, whereas now each one is active in the church.

Heavenly Father, I thank You for all Your blessings and all the ways that You have prospered me. Lord, teach me to guard my heart so that nothing will hinder my times of fellowship with You. Forgive me for the many times that the busyness of life has crowded out my time of prayer with You. Fill me with Your Spirit daily so that my times of prayer will be saturated with the richness of Your presence. Above anything else in life I want to hear Your voice and be sensitive to Your Spirit. Deepen my relationship with You so that I may fall more and more in love with You, and so that my greatest joy in life will be the times I spend with You in prayer. Teach me to rest in Your presence. Thank You that You will do all this and more! Amen.

"Trust in the Lord with all your heart; do not depend on your own understanding. Seek His will in all you do, and He will show you which path to take."
—*Proverbs 3:5-6,* NLT

In our relationship with the Son, we must pass the faithfulness to the vision test. This relates to the overall priority test because when our priorities are wrong then we will seek the wrong goals and not be faithful to the ultimate vision, which is Jesus Christ. In this test, sometimes our situation appears to be turned upside down or going in an unexpected direction. The temptation is to lean on our understanding instead of focusing on Jesus and trusting Him through times of apparent confusion.

An example of this test in my life happened a number of years after the Monday night Bible study had begun. I was in Mexico City at a ministers' conference in March, 2001. At one of the prayer meetings someone had a vision for me. The person saw an hourglass with sand pouring through it and a house in the top half of the glass. Then the house fell into the bottom half. Then the word GROWTH appeared.

The person had no idea what the vision meant but as soon as I heard it I immediately felt it referred to the Monday night Bible study, which was being held in our home. The time was coming when it must end. Initially I was very much resistant to the possibility of it ending. The Bible study was vibrant and the highlight of my week, even more than the Sunday morning church services. I didn't understand what the word GROWTH meant in regard to ending the Bible study. When I arrived back home I shared the vision and what I felt its interpretation was with our church elders. Their reaction was similar to mine in that they were reluctant to envision a time that the Monday night meetings would end.

A year passed and I went to a Christian convention in Texas in March, 2002. The Lord showed someone a vision that pertained to me and to the church in London. The person saw me in a spiritual battle. Part way through the battle I realized that I was wearing the wrong helmet. At first I did not want to change it because it was working but then I replaced it with the correct helmet. The person who had the vision felt that the helmet represented strategy. I had no idea what this vision meant.

By the end of March I began to notice something had changed in the Monday night Bible study which I couldn't identify. The elders sensed exactly the same thing. Attendance was down slightly but we were still averaging 50 to 60 people each week. I sensed that the time had come for the meetings to end but I was still resistant. I felt comfortable with its format and over the years the meetings had proven very fruitful. The church itself was birthed through the Monday night Bible study. I began to ask, "Lord, show me what You want to do in place of the Monday night meetings." I received no answer. Weeks passed and I continued to feel that now was the time to end the meetings but I didn't want to make a change until I knew what the next step was.

When I woke up one Monday morning at the end of June, 2002, and got out of bed, I felt a totally empty feeling when I thought of that evening's meeting. Then I remembered the vision from a few months before. The original helmet, which I had been wearing in the vision, represented the strategy God had given us, which was the Monday night meetings. However, the time had come that the Lord wanted to give us a new strategy, represented by the new helmet. But before I could put on the new helmet *I had to take off the old one.* I needed to end the Monday night Bible study. I realized my goal was wrong. The faithfulness to the vision test tests our loyalty to Jesus Christ. He is the purpose for all things. My loyalty had shifted to the meeting and my confidence was in the success of the Monday night Bible study.

When the Lord began to show me that the time had come to end the Monday night meetings I felt a lack of peace and even a sense of confusion. I felt like that clay vessel—turned upside down so it could be engraved with the master's initials. The situation was a total contradiction in my mind. However, that morning it became clear what I must do. The Lord would not reveal His next step until I obeyed His first step of drawing the Bible study to a close—even if it didn't make any sense to me. As soon as I decided this would be the last Bible study, a peace came over me. I phoned each of the elders and they too had the same witness.

After seven and a half years, the Bible study came to an end. We estimated that over 22,000 people had come to our home during that time. Every week new people would spontaneously walk through our door to attend the Bible study. It was amazing. It was never a strain on my wife, my children, or me that every Monday night the house was filled with people. Because of Lena's gift of hospitality, she willingly accepted the weekly invasion with grace and joy. My children accepted it as a normal part of their lives. And equally amazing, we felt no sense of loss, nostalgia, or any feeling of emptiness when it ended. We sensed that the Lord had accomplished what He intended through those meetings, and that this season of our lives had drawn to a close.

Something else happened unexpectedly. In four years, the church had grown at a very slow pace. We began with about 65 people in 1998, and by 2002 we still had fewer than 100 people. Within a few months after the Monday night meetings ended, new people began to come to the church. The new people were not in any way connected to the Monday night Bible study. For some reason, the church began to grow even though nothing else had changed. By mid-October, we were close to 120 people and within a year, we were running over 200 people, and the church was filled each Sunday morning. Then I remembered the one word I had not understood about the vision of the hourglass. That word was GROWTH.

As we keep our focus on Jesus Christ and He remains our goal and purpose, then we will pass the faithfulness to the vision test. Even when the Lord leads us in a direction that may appear not to make sense, or when we find ourselves in circumstances that seem to contradict everything we have come to trust—we will not be thrown off course but continue to keep our eyes on the author and finisher of our faith—Jesus Christ.

Heavenly Father, I thank You that You bring times in my life where things seem totally confusing so that my trust and focus will be on Your Son, Jesus Christ, and Him alone. Forgive me for the many times that I have failed and focused my eyes on the circumstances instead of my devotion to Jesus. Strengthen me so that during those times of testing, Your Spirit will rise up within me to fix my eyes fully on my Savior. Cause me to be an example to other believers so that they too can be strengthened and more dedicated to serving You. I praise You Lord for Your faithfulness and I believe that You are going to make me steadfast in the faith of the Son of God—independent of what is happening around me. Amen.

"If anyone speaks, he should do it as one speaking the very Words of God. If anyone serves, he should do it with the strength God provides, so that in all things God may be praised through Jesus Christ. To Him be the glory and the power for ever and ever. Amen."—1 Peter 4:11, NIV

In our relationship with the Holy Spirit we must pass the grace test. This relates to the overall priority test because when our priorities are properly ordered we are totally dependent upon the leading and empowerment of the Holy Spirit. Our confidence is to be in the Holy Spirit and nothing else. *"For we are the circumcision, who worship God in the Spirit, rejoice in Christ Jesus, and have no confidence in the flesh."* (Philippians 3:3).

An example of this test occurred on my first trip to Romania and Ukraine in 1994.

Before I begin the story I must fill in a bit of background. Soon after I received Christ as my Savior I began attending a Russian Pentecostal church that was near our home. Even though I did not even understand a word of Russian I felt very warmly received—maybe everyone wants at least one Jewish believer in their congregation. Within a few years, I had met Lena at the church and within two more years, we were married. Besides being very beautiful, she is also fluent in Russian. She was born in Australia but her mother was Russian and her father Polish, and she had grown up in the Russian Pentecostal church. I began to learn Russian, but not having a facility for foreign languages it was a slow and painful process. Science was my strength and not languages. That was one of the reasons I had gone into engineering. When you live in a country where a language is spoken, it is easier to learn that language, but my exposure to Russian was limited to church services. Yet after many years, I was able to carry on some level of conversation and read from the Bible. Given the amount of time I spent trying to learn Russian, others could well have been learning their third language. It never really flowed for me.

As I was preparing to fly to Austria to meet Robert Ewing, with whom I was to travel to Romania and on to Ukraine, my wife continued to warn me, "He thinks you're going to be his translator." I repeatedly reassured her that was not the case. In fact, I had told Robert several times that my Russian was poor and that I was not able to translate. Lena continued to insist that she thought he was looking to me to translate.

When I landed in Austria, I met a good friend who had just returned from Romania and was preparing to fly back to the United States. As we fellowshipped, he told me that Robert had told everyone that his translator was arriving that very day. I asked him who that was and my friend looked at me and said—"You!" To say I was shocked would be a gross understatement. I reassured my friend that he must be mistaken since Robert clearly knew that I was not a translator. He just smiled at me and said, "I am just telling you what Robert said." My reply was, "God can do anything, even raise someone from the dead or have me act as a Russian translator. But of those two miracles the second one would be more astounding." There were two things that I did not realize when I made that statement. The first was that one of the members of the team going with us to Romania had been miraculously raised from the dead when he was three years old. The second thing I didn't know was that I was indeed going to be the translator when we crossed over into Ukraine during the second half of our mission trip.

I spoke to Robert to try to convince him that there was a misunderstanding and that I was not a translator. He just smiled at me and said, "Praise the Lord. God will help you." I was thinking that the Lord was going to have to help a lot more people than just me. I phoned my wife and told her what was happening. My wife who is always there to encourage me in even the most difficult moments said only two things: "I told you so," and "You need to get on a plane and come back home right now." My wife, who had tried over the years to teach me Russian, knew my lack of fluency in the language. She was very concerned about the whole situation and I joined her in that concern.

I began to feel anxious. But then I thought to myself, *This is an opportunity to trust God, even though in the natural I feel totally incapable of doing what is required.* I remembered the prophetic words I had received concerning this trip, which really made me feel that the Lord's hand would be with me. This is really the grace test, when we cannot rely upon our own abilities but must totally trust the Holy Spirit to give us the grace to fulfill God's will. I decided to step out in faith. A team of seven of us went into Romania. We had Romanian translators and our meetings went smoothly. This first leg of the trip lasted ten days and then Robert, another Christian minister and I were to cross over into Ukraine from Romania for another ten days, and eventually work our way to Kiev where we would catch a plane to take us home.

As our time in Romania passed, thoughts about our trip into Ukraine tried to oppress me but I just kept putting the situation into God's hands. What made it even more challenging was that there were very few English-speaking people in the part of Ukraine we were entering. Even the government officials and border guards spoke only Ukrainian or Russian.

Soon the day came when we were to take the bus to the border. Half jokingly and half seriously I could see the headlines: "Two Americans and one Canadian lost in Ukraine. No trace of them has been found." We might spend the rest of our lives searching for directions to exit the country.

As we approached the border, the guard asked me a few questions and I was able to answer him. To my amazement we were able to communicate fairly well—to the point that I was able to secure entrance visas for the three of us. As we entered Ukraine, we were greeted by a

Ukrainian pastor who had been waiting for us. For the next ten days, all communication between Robert and anyone else passed through me. I was amazed at how fluent my Russian was; it wasn't perfect but it was understandable.

In Kiev, Robert was preaching in a fairly large church where they provided a translator—*praise the Lord!* However, as Robert began to teach on *The Seven Rest Principles*, the translator was losing the key points of his message. After about five minutes I told Robert that what he was teaching and what the translator was saying didn't line up. Robert asked me to straighten it out. I stood up and explained what Robert had just said. After I finished explaining the point, I was about to sit down when Robert said, "I believe that you are to teach this message." The translator sat down, Robert sat down, and there I stood at the front of the church. As I began to teach, the presence of the Lord began to manifest. I spoke for about 25 minutes. When I finished many were weeping, and the pastor himself was weeping. The pastor turned to me and asked if I could minister the next night as well. My Russian was far from perfect but through God's grace, the message not only flowed but God touched many hearts.

God used me in a way I would never have dreamed possible. Since that time I have made numerous trips to Russia. Trusting in God's provision and having no confidence in the flesh best summarize the grace test.

Heaven Father, I thank You for Your gift of the Holy Spirit. He is such a wonderful Comforter to me. Help me to always remember what a wonderful gift Your Spirit is, and that I should constantly turn to Him for guidance, comfort, and power. I earnestly desire the spiritual gifts to operate in me more powerfully. Cause the gifts of Your Spirit to flow more freely through me. I want to experience Your supernatural power on a daily basis. I want to be used by You in signs, wonders, and miracles that Jesus Christ may be glorified and that the truth of Your Word would be evident to all. Amen.

OUR RELATIONSHIP WITH THE GLORY OF GOD
The Faith Test

The seventh essential relationship is our relationship with the glory of God, and the corresponding test is the faith test. There are four glories of God, four corresponding faith tests, and four possible errors to be avoided in each faith test.

THE FOUR TYPES OF FAITH IN ABRAHAM'S LIFE

In Romans 4:17-22, we can see the four types of faith demonstrated in the life of Abraham—in fact the central theme of his life *is* faith. As the story of Abraham unfolds, we witness his struggles and his ultimate triumph as the Spirit of God takes an ordinary man and transforms him into a person of unwavering confidence in God. As we see throughout Scripture, God uses ordinary people to achieve extraordinary feats.

CREATIVE FAITH

> *"...(as it is written, "I have made you a father of many nations") in the presence of Him whom he believed—God, who gives life to the dead and calls those things which do not exist as though they did"*—Romans 4:17.

Abraham faced a mountain of natural circumstances that made it impossible for him to have a son—and that mountain was Sarah's age and her barren womb. Sarah's body was unable to create the promised son. In verse 17 we see that Abraham *believed* God, and his faith released into Abraham's life the creative power of God. Abraham did not stop at believing *in* God—Abraham *believed God*—and the words God had spoken. Because Abraham chose to believe God the creative power of God brought life to the deadness of Sarah's womb and called into existence what had not existed—the son of promise—Isaac. Creative faith can only be manifest when we are faced with impossible circumstances in the natural realm.

How often we accept God's promise, but like Abraham, take things into our own hands, to work out the details and timing *our* way. As believers, we must learn to embrace the promises of God in our darkest moments so that we can see the glory of His light appear and watch as He creates a glorious result from an impossible situation. Often we would prefer to withdraw from situations that challenge our faith, but God chooses those moments to teach us to operate in creative faith and call forth those things that do not exist.

DOCTRINAL FAITH

> *"...who, contrary to hope, in hope believed, so that he became the father of many nations, according to what was spoken, "So shall your descendants be."*—Romans 4:18

This verse describes how Abraham passed the doctrinal faith test. Abraham had two reports to consider. One report was from the natural point of view—the certain impossibility of Sarah ever being able to bear him a son. From the human point of view there was no hope. That fact became more evident each day as Sarah and Abraham grew well into old age—Abraham was one hundred years old and Sarah was ninety—well beyond childbearing age. The second report was from God Himself as He repeatedly confirmed to Abraham that he would have a son—*and through Sarah.*

Although Abraham knew that God could do anything, what he had to believe was that God would be faithful to fulfill what He had promised. Abraham had a choice to make. Would he choose to listen as his natural circumstances shouted, "You'll *never* have a child by Sarah!" Or would he choose to believe God's promise that he *would* have a child by Sarah? Had he chosen to develop his doctrine based on his past experiences or the wisdom of man, his doctrine would have been totally devoid of power and he would have failed to see God's promises fulfilled in his life. Abraham, through faith, chose to believe the Word of God and his doctrine was founded on God's Word, spoken to him. Abraham's hope was in God. Our beliefs need to line up with God's Word and not be based on our present circumstances or on our past experiences, failures, or even our successes.

PERSEVERING FAITH

> *"And not being weak in faith, he did not consider his own body, already dead (since he was about a hundred years old), and the deadness of Sarah's womb. He did not waver at the promise of God through unbelief, but was strengthened in faith, giving glory to God, and being fully convinced that what He had promised He was also able to perform."*

In verses 19-21 we see a brief description of Abraham's journey as he learned to walk in persevering faith. His chosen path was not always smooth and there were times when he doubted and struggled to fully trust God. Because of Abraham's temporary unbelief, he fathered a child, Ishmael, by Sarah's servant Hagar. As he lost hope, he even went into Egypt where he lied about Sarah being his wife. *Our actions always reflect what we believe.* But through all those barren and fruitless years God was with Abraham to correct him, teach him, and ultimately to commend him for becoming a man of faith—one who chose to believe God rather than his natural circumstances. Abraham learned not to waver at the promises of God through unbelief. Instead he was strengthened in his faith and brought glory to God and to His Word.

GOD-CONSCIOUS FAITH

"And therefore "it was accounted to him for righteousness."

Verse 22 provides a beautiful description of the conclusion of Abraham's life *"...it was accounted to him for righteousness."* This speaks about the right relationship that Abraham had with God through faith and that he was able to speak to God as a friend. James describes his relationship with God this way: *"You see that his faith and his actions were working together, and his faith was made complete by what he did. Abraham believed God, and it was credited to him as righteousness, and he was called God's friend."* (James 2:22-23b, NIV). God's friend—this speaks about God-conscious faith and a consistent and intimate walk with God. When we are confident of our righteous standing in Christ, we have boldness in our relationship with Him and we are able to develop God-conscious faith. Believers who are not confident in God's unconditional love and acceptance are unable to see God as their friend, and maintaining fellowship with God becomes a wearisome chore. But when we learn to walk with God, our greatest desire is to experience more of God. He both creates and satisfies a hunger and thirst for Him.

THE FOUR TYPES OF ERROR

The following verses illustrate a link and a progression between the four types of error—error of vision, error of doctrine, error of lifestyle, and error of attitude.

> *"If anyone wills to do His will, he shall know concerning the doctrine, whether it is from God or whether I speak on My own authority. He who speaks from himself seeks his own glory; but He who seeks the glory of the One who sent Him is true, and no unrighteousness is in Him. Did not Moses give*

you the law, yet none of you keeps the law? Why do you seek to kill Me?"—John 7:17-19.

ERROR OF VISION

"He who speaks from himself seeks his own glory."—John 7:18a.

This verse illustrates the error that leads to wrong motivation. We have entered into the error of vision when we draw glory to ourselves, our leaders, or anyone or anything else. Our true purpose is to glorify God's name and not to draw glory to ourselves, and our full loyalty must be to God Himself—He must be our first priority. Jesus Himself said, *"If I honor Myself, My honor is nothing. It is My Father who honors Me, of whom you say that He is your God."* (John 8:54). The same might be said of us. Jesus asked, *"How can you believe, who receive honor from one another, and do not seek the honor that comes from the only God?"* (John 5:44). We need to ask ourselves whose honor we would prefer—man's glory or God's glory. God said *"...My glory I will not give to another"*—God alone is due all honor and glory. (Isaiah 42:8a).

Paul described this part of their downward spiral as follows: *"...although they knew God, they did not glorify Him as God..."* (Romans 1:21a). An error of vision causes us to have the wrong motive, which in turn deprives us of the ability to discern false doctrine. Our focus has ceased to be on God; it has turned inward to focus on ourselves. When our focus is diverted from God, we are no longer correctible and such an attitude leads us into errors of doctrine.

ERROR OF DOCTRINE

"If anyone wills to do His will, he shall know concerning the doctrine, whether it is from God or whether I speak on My own authority."—John 7:17.

This verse provides us with the key to discerning between false doctrine and true doctrine so that we will not fall into error. Anyone who desires to do the will of God will know and be able to perceive doctrine that is truly from God. The error of doctrine is not rooted in any wrong idea we might happen to believe. The root lies in impure motivation in our heart, which impairs our ability to discern between what is of God and what is not of God. We may be bound by pride, false desires, and false loyalties to our culture, religion, or family—or a host of other obstacles, which take the place of truly wanting to know God and His truth.

Paul described such persons as follows: *"...who exchanged the truth of God for the lie..."* (Romans 1:25a). If there is rebellion and selfishness in our heart, we will prefer our will over God's will, and our true motivation will not be to do God's will but to serve ourselves.

ERROR OF LIFESTYLE

"Did not Moses give you the law, yet none of you keeps the law?"—John 7:19a.

Jesus spoke in verse 19 of the error of doctrine that leads to error of lifestyle. The message the Pharisees preached was steeped in legalism because they were totally blind to the mercy and grace of God. Although they taught others how to keep the law to be holy, they themselves were unable to keep the very law they taught. They taught but failed to live the truth and the result was an error of lifestyle. In Matthew, Chapter 23, the seven woes pronounced by Jesus were directed to the teachers of the law and the Pharisees, as He repeatedly referred to them as hypocrites. Theirs was very much a message of do as I say, not as I do—a lifestyle of total hypocrisy.

Paul noted this error in Romans 1:28, *"And even as they did not like to retain God in their knowledge, God gave them over to a debased mind to do those things which are not fitting."* Their vision was wrong—they did not retain God in their thoughts and their wrong thoughts led to wrong life choices. Paul describes some of these wrong lifestyle practices in verses 29-31: *"being filled with all unrighteousness, sexual immorality, wickedness, covetousness, maliciousness, full of envy, murder, strife, deceit, evil-mindedness; they are whisperers, backbiters, haters of God, violent, proud, boasters, inventors of evil things, disobedient to parents, undiscerning, untrustworthy, unloving, unforgiving, unmerciful."* They were now unable to discern what was from God and what was not. Their wrong vision and beliefs were now put into action as deeds—errors of lifestyle.

ERROR OF ATTITUDE

"Why do you seek to kill Me?"—John 7:19b.

Errors of lifestyle eventually—like a poison—corrupt the entire person and produce an error of spirit or attitude. We see this described in the last part of verse 19. The legalistic doctrine of the Pharisees led them into error of lifestyle that prevented them from receiving the grace and mercy of God to live a truly pure and holy life. But beyond that, their wrong doctrine caused bitterness and hatred to enter their hearts until they were filled with murderous thoughts against Jesus. The Pharisees' successive errors of vision, doctrine, lifestyle, and attitude ultimately led them to crucify the Lord Jesus. Rather than put their own sins to death, they put to death the very One who is the way, the truth, and the life, and who died for their sins.

Paul described such an attitude in Romans 1:21b-22 as *"...nor were thankful, but became futile in their thoughts and their foolish hearts were darkened. Professing to be wise, they became fools..."* Paul ends this chapter by saying, *"They know God's justice requires that those who do these things deserve to die, yet they do them anyway,"* demonstrating an attitude of willful and flagrant rebellion against God. (Romans 1:32, NLT). Their hearts were hardened toward God, to the point of promoting in others the ungodly lifestyle choices they practiced. The Message phrases this verse in contemporary language: *"They know perfectly well they're spitting in God's face. And they don't care—worse, they hand out prizes to those who do the worst things best."* This is the ultimate end result of error of attitude—a complete lack of God-consciousness and total depravity. Even believers can harden their hearts until their attitude is one of contempt and rebellion against God.

THE FOUR TYPES OF ERROR IN SAMSON'S LIFE

Samson is an example of someone who descended deeply into error. The Lord had called him to be a Nazirite—consecrated unto the Lord from his mother's womb. The calling on Samson's life was to be a judge, a deliverer, and an example to God's people. He was given a special anointing to overcome Israel's enemies, but instead of glorifying the name of the Lord and drawing the people's hearts closer to God, he glorified himself and became a folk hero. Samson fell into the error of vision because of his self-centered attitude.

The strength God had given him allowed him to defeat the Philistines, but his only motivation for fighting them was pride, impulsive anger, and self-exaltation. Samson's heart was never stirred by the plight of his people nor did he express his gratitude to God for the gift and calling upon his life. Samson's victories over the Philistines did not stir Israel to praise God nor did it cause their faith to grow. Samson directed the people's attention to himself and not to the Lord.

Samson's doctrine or philosophy of life was "let us eat, drink, and be merry today for tomorrow we die." He lived to satisfy the desires of his flesh, completely devoid of eternal perspective. The concept of restraint and self-control was foreign to his thinking. Because he neither valued God's Word nor studied it, he fell into error of doctrine. His life became one aimless pursuit of fleshly pleasure.

Samson's error of doctrine clearly led him into error of lifestyle. His lustful and unrestrained desires dominated his words and conduct and set the course of his life on a downward spiral. His lifestyle of fornication and self-will ultimately caused him to fall into the enemy's trap and he was blinded, imprisoned, and forced to work as a slave.

Before Samson was captured by the Philistines, we can clearly see his error of spirit or attitude. He had no regard for God or His Word. He lacked any fear of God and his haughty attitude led him to do whatever he wished.

Although Samson wasted his life and pursued selfish lusts, God began to speak to him as he sat in that Philistine prison—blind and weak. The Bible does not offer specific details of his prison experience, but clearly God was working in Samson's heart to restore his inner life and fulfill his purpose. As Samson lost his physical eyesight he gained spiritual insight. Finally he recognized the Philistines for who they really were—they had drawn his soul senses into the carnal realm—and he had allowed carnal pursuits to blind him. They diverted his focus from God to follow fleshly desires.

One day the Philistines brought Samson out to mock both him and the God of Israel, but now Samson's heart was right with God. He was no longer impulsive and self-willed. It was a transformed Samson who leaned with one hand on each of the temple's main supporting pillars. Samson's prayer to God was not rash or selfish but was filled with reverence, humility, and faith. *"Then Samson called to the Lord, saying, 'O Lord God, remember me, I pray! Strengthen me, I pray, just this once. O God, that I may with one blow take vengeance on the Philistines for my two eyes!'"* (Judges 16:28). He looked to God for his strength. He was willing to die to defeat God's enemies—whom he now recognized as his enemies. The Philistines had robbed him of his eyesight, and now he wanted to destroy those who mocked God and diverted him from God's purpose—now his will was conformed to God's will. As he pushed down the two supporting pillars, the temple crumbled. He overcame his own flesh and destroyed God's enemies—but at the cost of his own life.

Samson had been seduced by the world. *"For all that is in the world—the lust of the flesh, the lust of the eyes, and the pride of life—is not of the Father but is of the world."* (1 John 2:16). We, like Samson, must reckon ourselves dead to sin so that we can live with Christ and identify with His crucifixion. The Philistines are a metaphor for those temptations in our lives that sidetrack us into the worldly realm, where our focus is on the temporal rather than the eternal prospective.

In his death he killed more of Israel's enemies than he had in his life. Samson's one act of unselfish obedience had a greater impact on the nation of Israel than anything else he had done. But the most astounding thing about Samson is not found in the Old Testament, but is written about him in the New Testament. Samson is named among those in the great hall of fame of faith in Hebrews, Chapter 11. Samson is counted among the Old Testament saints who were found faithful! Ultimately Samson passed the faith test and restored his relationship with God's glory.

TWO TYPES OF SUFFERING

Samson certainly endured much suffering on his journey to restoration, but unlike Joseph, his painful experiences were not part of God's plan. Samson's suffering was self-inflicted—as a direct consequence of his wrong choices. In the lives of these two men we observe two types of suffering. Joseph suffered because he hungered and thirsted for righteousness, Samson suffered as the result of wrong personal choices.

The pain experienced by Samson need not have occurred. But the wonderful thing about God's grace is that He is able to use both types of suffering to bring about His ultimate purpose. This is the underlying principle of Romans 8:28. For many years Samson resisted the call and leading of the Holy Spirit, which caused him to *"fall into temptation and a snare, and into many foolish and harmful lusts which drown men in destruction and perdition."* (1 Timothy 6:9b). However, the Lord did not leave Samson in that condition. His Spirit visited Samson while he was confined to prison—a prison of his own making. Joseph and Samson spent time in prison for different reasons—Joseph as a result of his desire to walk with the Lord—and Samson because he chose to walk his own way. Samson's suffering would have been more intense because he had to overcome the shame and guilt of his rebellion, receive the Lord's forgiveness, and learn to forgive himself. The final victory in Samson's life resulted from his ultimate submission to God. Both men learned to trust God's grace before they were removed from their respective prisons. Their choices impacted their lives in two very different ways. Samson fulfilled God's call, but paid dearly—with his life, while Joseph was groomed for greatness because he passed each of God's tests. Joseph died to himself and lived—Samson lived for himself and died.

Our God is a God of restoration and redemption. No matter how far we fall He is always there to pick us up and walk with us through the process of restoration and redemption.

COMPLETION OF THE CLAY VESSEL

In the seventh stage, the clay vessel is ready for its final firing. This is not the first exposure of the clay vessel to the heat of the kiln. In the third part of the sixth essential relationship, which is our relationship with the Holy Spirit, the vessel received its initial firing. At that time, the clay vessel contained moisture, carbon, and other impurities.

In the initial firing, at first the temperature was kept very low. The water remaining in the clay had to be evaporated off below the boiling point or the generated steam would cause the vessel to explode. As the temperature of the kiln slowly increased, carbon and other impurities were released. As the kiln temperature further increased, the clay particles were chemically altered—they became cemented together forming a permanently hard product. The initial firing set the shape, hardened and strengthened the vessel, and caused irreversible changes in the clay.

In our relationship with the Holy Spirit, as mentioned earlier, the test we must pass is the grace test. This occurred when we were baptized with the Holy Spirit and fire. We only learn to rely on God's grace when the heat is turned up, so to speak. It is only when our natural abilities and resources are insufficient that we can learn to totally trust in the Holy Spirit. Grace can be defined as God working in us and through us to accomplish His purposes. The Lord walks us through experiences where we see His grace accomplishing wonderful things that we know on our own we would be incapable of accomplishing. Some would describe such experiences as "being stretched." We are not necessarily brought to a point of desperation, but to a point of needing to rely on God's grace. As we learn to be led by the Holy Spirit, we see Him bring about wonders such as healings, miracles, amazing answers to prayer, and the transformation of lives.

To pass the grace test we must rely fully on God's grace and put no confidence in the flesh. Paul described his relationship with the grace of God, *"And He said to me, "My grace is sufficient for you, for My strength is made perfect in weakness." Therefore most gladly I will rather boast in my infirmities, that the power of Christ may rest upon me."* (2 Corinthians 12:9). The initial firing can be seen as a time when we learn to trust in His grace and not in our strength. This might be compared to a soldier training in war games. The soldier experiences some of the realities of war and its stresses, learning how to use his equipment without the full weight of an actual battle, while the final firing could be compared to the same soldier later in the heat of actual combat.

The final firing is carried out at a considerably hotter kiln temperature. The degree of hardness and strength of the final vessel depend on the intensity of the heat during the final firing. The greater the heat, the stronger the resulting vessel. At Calvary, Jesus endured the ultimate heat as He became a burnt offering as the perfect Lamb of God. *"For it was fitting for Him, for whom are all things and by whom are all things, in bringing many sons to glory, to make the captain of their salvation perfect through sufferings."* (Hebrews 2:10).

In the final firing, the full weight of our circumstances may try to crush us and it is during that time that our faith can rise up to overcome our circumstances and bring glory to God. Faith can only be seen operating when everything else is impossible. In the great faith chapter of Hebrews 11, we see example after example of men and women of faith overcoming impossible circumstances—some even facing a martyr's death, all the while maintaining a good confession of God's faithfulness.

The correct temperature is essential in both firings, and required great experience, judgment, and skill on the part of the ancient potter. Too much heat during the initial firing would destroy the vessel and too little heat during the final firing would result in an inferior vessel.

In relationship to the four aspects of God's Glory, we see how the intensity of impossibilities increases in each successive step beginning with creative faith, moving into doctrinal faith, and then the weight of increasing pressures of circumstance in persevering faith, and ultimately being able to face any danger through God-conscious faith. Jesus never promised His children that they would never face danger or even martyrdom, but He did say that we are to be of good courage because He has overcome the world. God is asking us to trust Him and He will give us such faith and confidence that we will be able to face even death.

Whether we live in countries where Christians are persecuted for their faith or in countries where there is religious freedom, we will all have to face death. I once heard it said that the true faith of a person is not seen in how they lived but in how they died. When we have that ultimate God-conscious faith, then even the greatest enemy of man—death—cannot move us. The book of second Timothy describes the Apostle Paul as he faced martyrdom. Not only was he unmoved by his impending death but he looked forward with joy to being with the Lord.

GOD'S GLORY REVEALED IN JOSEPH'S LIFE

As Joseph was summoned and stood before Pharaoh it is difficult to imagine the pressure trying to crush his soul. Why did Pharaoh want to see Joseph? There was a great deal at stake—Joseph could be released, returned to prison, or executed. When Joseph heard what was required of him and Pharaoh's expectation, more pressure was placed upon him. And as he told Pharaoh what God had spoken, how would Pharaoh respond to hearing that a seven-year famine was coming? If Joseph failed to answer Pharaoh correctly or if Pharaoh didn't like the interpretation, Joseph could have been subjected to further imprisonment or even death. *The rulers in those days were sometimes fickle, and often killed the messenger.*

Joseph had passed each of the previous tests and he was now ready to face his greatest test with the faith God had cultivated in his heart, revealing the glory of God. Just as the clay is transformed from a shapeless lump into a beautiful vessel fit for use, Joseph was also transformed from a simple believer at the age of seventeen into one who knew His God intimately. At thirty years of age he stood before Pharaoh ready to be tested and proven—he was now a vessel fit for the Master's use!

The psalmist outlines how God reversed Joseph's circumstances. *"Moreover He called for a famine in the land; He destroyed all the provision of bread. He sent a man before them—Joseph—who was sold as a slave. They hurt his feet with fetters, he was laid in irons. Until the time that his word came to pass, the word of the LORD tested him. The king sent and released him, the ruler of the people let him go free. He made him lord of his house, and ruler of all his possessions, to bind his princes at his pleasure, and teach his elders wisdom."* (Psalm 105:16-22). God ordained every circumstance that Joseph went through. Joseph was separated from his family, sold into slavery, falsely accused by Potiphar's wife and thrown into prison by Potiphar, even the famine—all these incidents were ordained by God. Why? They prepared Joseph to receive God's glory as he gave up control of his own destiny and fully embraced God's will.

Joseph held onto God's Word, given as a prophetic promise in his childhood dream, and the dream was ultimately fulfilled. The dream that portrayed his brothers' sheaves bowing down to Joseph was the same dream that evoked such hatred and resentment in his brothers. In the dream, God used the symbolism of grain to illustrate Joseph's future relationship with his brothers, a picture of sheaves of grain, bowing down before his sheaf. And it was precisely the lack of grain in Canaan and the abundance of grain in Egypt that reunited him with his brothers and his father.

Because seven years of famine lay ahead for Canaan, Joseph's family moved to Egypt where Joseph ruled over them as governor of Egypt. His father's response to his dream *"Shall your mother and I and your brothers indeed come to bow down to the earth before you?"* was also prophetic. (Genesis 37:10). Indeed, *"Judah and his brothers came to Joseph's house, and he was still there; and they fell before him* (Joseph) *on the ground."* (Genesis 44:14). His brother's submission before Joseph is mentioned several times in the story, *"And they bowed their heads down and prostrated themselves."* (Genesis 43:28b). *"And when Joseph came home, they brought him the present which was in their hand into the house, and bowed down before him to the earth."* (Genesis 43:26).

Joseph understood the purpose his suffering served. He saw from God's perspective how his separation from his family, his subsequent sale into slavery, and wrongful imprisonment, eventually lead to the deliverance of not only Joseph's own family but all of Egypt and Israel from the famine. This is clearly evident in these verses: *"And God sent me before you to preserve a posterity for you in the earth, and to save your lives by a great deliverance. So now it was not you who sent me here, but God; and He has made me a father to Pharaoh, and lord of all his house, and a ruler throughout all the land of Egypt."* (Genesis 45:7-8). *"But as for you, you meant evil against me; but God meant it for good, in order to bring it about as it is this day, to save many people alive."* (Genesis 50:20).

God made a promise to Jacob. He changed Jacob's name to Israel, and promised a great nation would emanate from him. God had a purpose—to save Jacob's family from the coming famine. God had a plan—to fulfill His promise to Jacob the father, through Joseph the son. God's plan was to promote Joseph to a position of power in Egypt, where he could prepare for the famine during the years of abundant crops. God had a process—to cause Joseph to fully enter into the seven essential relationships with God so that His promise, purpose, and plan could all be fulfilled to bring glory to God.

From Joseph's dream to its fruition, God used Joseph to advance and bring about His promises to Jacob. *"All the persons of the house of Jacob who went to Egypt were seventy."* (Genesis 46:27b). The nation of Israel was born from those seventy members of Jacob's family. The meaning of the name *Joseph* is "to add, to increase," and it was because of Joseph that the Hebrew people were increased in number, the twelve tribes of Israel were preserved, and Israel was saved from destruction.

The story of Joseph speaks of the sovereignty of an omniscient God who planned long beforehand to bring Joseph to a position of power in Egypt where he could fulfill a divine purpose—for Joseph to rule over Egypt, prepare for the famine, save Jacob, his family, and all of Egypt from the famine. The story also beautifully illustrates the amazing and abundant fruit borne from one person's obedience and faithfulness to God. And through Joseph's testimony, God alone received the glory.

JOSEPH'S FORGIVENESS

When Joseph was reunited with his brothers, we can observe the depth of his forgiveness and his attitude toward his brothers. There were no recriminations, no blame, no angry words—nor did he demand an apology for their behavior. His relationship with his brothers was lovingly restored. *"Moreover he* (Joseph) *kissed all his brothers and wept over them, and after that his brothers talked with him."* (Genesis 45:15). When they saw how totally he had forgiven them and his loving attitude toward them, they were able to open their hearts to him. Joseph's heart was so pure that he could only weep with great joy over their reunion, and his great delight that his father, Jacob, was alive and well.

Joseph consoled and comforted them, even absolving them from any blame for what they had done. He said, *"But now, do not therefore be grieved or angry with yourselves because you sold me here; for God sent me before you to preserve life.*" (Genesis 45:5). Joseph's response so beautifully illustrates the words Paul spoke concerning forgiveness. "*So [instead of further rebuke, now] you should rather turn and [graciously] forgive and comfort and encourage [him], to keep him from being overwhelmed by excessive sorrow and despair. I therefore beg you to reinstate him in your affections and assure him of your love for him.*" (2 Corinthians 2:7-8, THE AMPLIFIED BIBLE). Joseph had realized his brothers were grieved over their actions when he overheard them speaking in what they thought was a private conversation.

Joseph then chose to bless his family. "*Bring your father and your households and come to me; I will give you the best of the land of Egypt, and you will eat the fat of the land.*" (Genesis 45:18). He provided the grain they so desperately needed, refused any payment, and invited them to live with him in Egypt. Joseph was acting out Peter's words: "*...having compassion for one another; love as brothers, be tenderhearted, be courteous; not returning evil for evil or reviling for reviling, but on the contrary blessing, knowing that you were called to this, that you may inherit a blessing.*" (1 Peter 3:8b-9). Joseph's complete forgiveness of his brothers brought about the restoration of his family, comfort and absolution for his brothers, blessing upon the whole house of Jacob, and God was glorified.

THE EFFECT OF JOSEPH'S FAITHFULNESS ON HIS FAMILY

His brothers had a calling on their lives to receive a revelation of God's glory as well, but it was Joseph who received the full revelation because he passed the necessary tests. However, Joseph's brothers and his whole family were all touched by Joseph's relationship with God.

What effect did Joseph's seven essential relationships with God have on his brothers? When they came to Egypt to buy food, Joseph accused them of being spies. "*It is as I spoke to you, saying, 'You are spies!' In this manner you shall be tested: By the life of Pharaoh, you shall not leave this place unless your youngest brother comes here. Send one of you, and let him bring your brother; and you shall be kept in prison, that your words may be tested to see whether there is any truth in you; or else, by the life of Pharaoh, surely you are spies!' So he put them all together in prison three days."* (Genesis 42:14b-17).

"Then they said to one another, 'We are truly guilty concerning our brother, for we saw the anguish of his soul when he pleaded with us, and we would not hear; therefore this distress has come upon us.' And Reuben answered them, saying, 'Did I not speak to you, saying, 'Do not sin against the boy;' and you would not listen? Therefore behold, his blood is now required of us.' But they did not know that Joseph understood them, for he spoke to them through an interpreter." (Genesis 42:21-23). His brothers recognized their circumstances were the direct result of their actions some thirteen years before, and they were now reaping what they had sown. They were convicted of their sin toward Joseph, and they confessed it before him, although they failed to recognize Joseph as their brother. Now God was calling Joseph's brothers into a relationship with The Way in Which He Deals With Us.

For the fourth time in the story *"Then his brothers also went and fell down before his face, and they said, Behold, we are your servants."* (Genesis 50:18). His brothers were now learning to be submissive to authority—authority embodied in their brother Joseph! How dramatically his brothers' opinion toward Joseph had changed. The last time they saw him, they so devalued his life that they sold him for twenty shekels of silver. Now their lives and those of their children were totally dependant on Joseph as ruler of Egypt and provider of the grain that would sustain them. Jacob and Joseph's brothers now had a relationship with Pharaoh, and Pharaoh made this promise to Joseph regarding them: *"The land of Egypt is before you. Have your father and brothers dwell in the best of the land; let them dwell in the land of Goshen."* (Genesis 47:6a). The meaning of the name *Goshen* means "to draw near" and Joseph's family drew near—not only to Joseph but to the king himself.

As Jacob and his family prospered in Egypt, all of God's promises were fulfilled. *"So Israel dwelt in the land of Egypt, in the country of Goshen; and they had possessions there and grew and multiplied exceedingly."* (Genesis 47:27).

How do we see Joseph's relationship with God's glory? Finally in the seventh relationship, Joseph related to God's glory by passing all four parts of the faith test: The Creative Faith Test, The Doctrinal Faith Test, The Persevering Faith Test, and The God-Conscious Faith Test.

THE GLORY OF GOD'S NAME– THE CREATIVE FAITH TEST

The first aspect of our relationship with the glory of God's name is the creative faith test. Creative faith is demonstrated by speaking into being things which are not. Romans 4:17 speaks of Abraham's creative faith by saying, *"...who gives life to the dead and calls those things which do not exist as though they did..."* We see this relationship played out as Joseph was called before Pharaoh. When Pharaoh had a dream that no one could interpret, the butler suddenly remembered how Joseph had correctly interpreted his dream in prison. Genesis 41:14-16 says, *"Then Pharaoh sent and called Joseph, and they brought him quickly out of the dungeon; and he shaved, changed his clothing, and came to Pharaoh. And Pharaoh said to Joseph, "I have had a dream, and there is no one who can interpret it. But I have heard it said of you that you can understand a dream, to interpret it. So Joseph answered Pharaoh, saying, 'It is not in me; God will give Pharaoh an answer of peace.'"*

Joseph went before Pharaoh and declared that the interpretation was not in him, but instead in God, and in doing so, he glorified God's name. By giving God the glory and taking no credit for himself, Joseph spoke into existence God's answer to Pharaoh. He didn't say, "Yeah, I'm pretty good at interpreting dreams." It was not in Joseph's heart to say that. Instead, he declared the glory of God's name. What was the creative faith test? Before Joseph even *heard* the dream, he said, *"God* will give Pharaoh an answer of peace." Most of us would have said, "Let me hear it first, and then I'll tell you what I think." Joseph had grown so confident in his relationship with the Holy Spirit that he stood with creative faith and said, "*God will* give Pharaoh an answer of peace."

The word *peace* is the Hebrew word *shalom* which has multiple meanings, but it can mean "safety, prosperity, wealth, and contentment." Not only was Joseph convinced that God would give Pharaoh *an* answer, he was also convinced that God's answer would bring *peace* to Pharaoh. The interpretation brought prosperity and safety to Israel. What a testimony of Joseph's faithfulness to God and of God's faithfulness to His chosen people! Joseph knew all the trials he had endured had come from the hand of God, yet Joseph trusted God's faithfulness to give Pharaoh *"an answer of peace."* Joseph was tremendously confident—his intimacy with God had produced not only an assurance of God's person but of His inherent goodness. How Joseph's faithfulness must have delighted the heart of God!

The error to be avoided in the creative faith test is the error of vision. The error of vision occurs when we attempt to speak our own desires into existence, and not words from God. Creative faith operates only when the Spirit of God speaks through us for the glory of God's name. Joseph passed the test correctly without an error of vision. The interpretation of Pharaoh's dream was for the glory of God's name—and not Joseph's name—and Joseph knew that very well. Joseph realized that he was only the vessel and not its creator. He could not interpret the dream, but knew that God would provide the interpretation as he rested in God's abilities and not his own. Joseph realized that God was the source of the wisdom to interpret the dream and he was not tempted to take any of the glory for himself, even when—to the utter astonishment of Pharaoh and his court—he gave the correct interpretation.

THE GLORY OF GOD'S WORD– THE DOCTRINAL FAITH TEST

The second aspect of God's glory is the glory of His Word. The corresponding test is the doctrinal faith test, and the possible error is the error of doctrine. It is a test of faith because we need the faith of Jesus within us to see the truth and to understand doctrine. Joseph had the correct interpretation to Pharaoh's dream, but he also had godly wisdom to supply the appropriate application of the revealed truth. He had learned to discern between the Word of God and his own thoughts, as he said with certainty, *"...the thing is established by God, and God will shortly bring it to pass."* (Genesis 41:32b). Not only was God's glory revealed by the correct interpretation of Pharaoh's dream, but God also revealed to Joseph the solution to the problem, and the correct course of action. God's will is always result oriented, always redemptive, and it always brings hope.

In prison Joseph held on to the Word of God through unfavorable circumstances. Now Joseph had to hold on to the Word of God during the seven plentiful years as he prepared for the coming famine. God tested Joseph's faith in His Word when circumstances appeared to be both unfavorable and favorable. He tested Joseph's stewardship when he had nothing of his own, and again when he lived in abundance as the second most powerful man in Egypt. And as he passed the test, Pharaoh and his servants marveled saying, *"Can we find such a one as this, a man in whom is the Spirit of God?"* (Genesis 41:38b). They recognized the glory of God's Word because Joseph had the Word of God, correct doctrine, correct interpretation, and the proper application. It is essential to recognize the authority of God's Word and to have correct understanding. The error of doctrine brings shame and disgrace to God's Word because the world sees teaching that is powerless, confusing, irrelevant, or untrue. God has given us His written Word, which is the foundation of all truth, and we must seek God for the correct understanding of the Scriptures.

THE GLORY OF GOD'S LIFE–
THE PERSEVERING FAITH TEST

The third aspect of this relationship is receiving the glory of God's life. The accompanying test is the persevering faith test and the possible error is the error of lifestyle. Pharaoh listened as Joseph told him about the coming famine. *"Indeed seven years of great plenty will come throughout all the land of Egypt; but after them seven years of famine will arise, and all the plenty will be forgotten in the land of Egypt; and the famine will deplete the land." "Now therefore, let Pharaoh select a discerning and wise man, and set him over the land of Egypt. Let Pharaoh do this, and let him appoint officers over the land, to collect one-fifth of the produce of the land of Egypt in the seven plentiful years."* (Genesis 41:29-30; 33-34).

Pharaoh's reply is recorded in verses 37-41. *"So the advice was good in the eyes of Pharaoh and in the eyes of all his servants. And Pharaoh said to his servants, 'Can we find such a one as this, a man in whom is the Spirit of God?' Then Pharaoh said to Joseph, 'Inasmuch as God has shown you all this, there is no one as discerning and wise as you. You shall be over my house, and all my people shall be ruled according to your word; only in regard to the throne will I be greater that you.' And Pharaoh said to Joseph, 'See, I have set you over all the land of Egypt.'"* It is significant that when Joseph gave the correct interpretation, those present realized that Joseph was truly submitted to the Spirit of God and that he was trustworthy—a man of unquestioned integrity. Pharaoh instantly installed Joseph into a position of responsibility because he saw the purity, power, and authority of God in Joseph.

Before installing Joseph as ruler over all of Egypt, one might have asked him one significant question: "I understand you were in prison, perhaps you could tell me a little about your background. Why were you in prison? Were you a murderer or a thief?" Most people would have liked to know more about this fellow, especially why he had spent so much time in prison. Would it not be a normal thing to ask for his resume or references? After all, in the space of one day, Joseph went from being a prisoner to becoming Pharaoh's administrator over all of Egypt, and the second most powerful man in the kingdom. But there was such integrity, so much of the life of God within Joseph, that regardless of his circumstances they saw a man led by the Spirit of God. They saw the perseverance of the life of God within Joseph, and they willingly accepted that he would be the ruler of Egypt, and agreed that no one could lift a finger without his permission.

Joseph's life is an amazing testimony of what God did first in his heart, then in his life, and finally affecting the lives of others. God prepared Joseph's heart, and formed godly character within him to fulfill the purpose for which he was called. Joseph had persevered through all his trials and when he stood before Pharaoh, the grace of God shone so powerfully that Pharaoh, without hesitation and with the full agreement of his court, chose Joseph to rule over Egypt. Because of Joseph's unquestioned integrity and submission to authority, he was promoted in each circumstance he faced—in Potiphar's household, in the prison, and finally by Pharaoh himself.

As we progress through these seven relationships, people will sense the glory of God, the purity, simplicity, and the love of Jesus within us, as the fruit of the Spirit increases in our lives. The persevering faith test can best be measured by watching a person over time. How do they relate to their spouse and their children? How do they respond when they are experiencing stress? How do they walk through trials? To pass this test, we must live a life of consistently believing in and yielding to God.

The error to be avoided in this test is the error of lifestyle. Often when pressures come, people buckle under them and fall into temptations such as immorality, greed, or other sin, which are errors of lifestyle. But there was no error of lifestyle in Joseph's life; they saw that Joseph walked in a lifestyle of integrity.

THE GLORY OF GOD'S PRESENCE –
THE GOD-CONSCIOUS FAITH TEST

The fourth aspect is the glory of God's presence and the accompanying faith test is one of God-consciousness. The error we can fall into is an error of attitude and unless we are God-conscious, we may develop a wrong attitude. When we have a consciousness of God, we will have an attitude of thanksgiving, an attitude of recognizing that God is with us regardless of how desperate our situation. This requires a very high level of spiritual maturity, but that is what God intends for us.

We see God's glory in Joseph's life in Genesis 41:42-45: *"Then Pharaoh took his signet ring off his hand and put it on Joseph's hand; and he clothed him in garments of fine linen and put a gold chain around his neck. And he had him ride in the second chariot which he had; and they cried out before him, 'Bow the knee!' So he set him over all the land of Egypt. Pharaoh also said to Joseph, 'I am Pharaoh, and without your consent no man may lift his hand or foot in all the land of Egypt.' And Pharaoh called Joseph's name Zaphnath-Paaneah. And he gave him as a wife Asenath, the daughter of Po-tiPherah priest of On. So Joseph went out over all the land of Egypt."* The Egyptian name that Joseph received means "treasury of the glorious rest," because Pharaoh recognized God's glorious presence was in him.

We can enter into God's rest now but this passage of Scripture also describes our relationship with God during the millennium. What an intimate gesture on the part of Pharaoh to place his ring on Joseph's finger, to clothe him in fine linen, to put a chain around his neck, and to have Joseph ride in the second chariot, right beside Pharaoh. Prophetically we see Pharaoh as a picture of God the Father exalting Jesus the Son through His position as ruler over all creation, seated at the right hand of the Father.

During the seven years while Joseph prepared for the coming famine, two sons were born to him. The first was called Manasseh. *"Joseph called the name of the firstborn Manasseh: 'For God has made me forget all my toil and all my father's house.'"* (Genesis 41:51). The name *Manasseh* means "to cause to forget." In the midst of Egypt, which had been a place of suffering for Joseph, God caused him to forget the pain. Revelation 21:4 says, *"And God will wipe away every tear from their eyes; there shall be no more death, nor sorrow, nor crying. There shall be no more pain, for the former things have passed away."* In God's presence we will forget our past pain and behold His glory as we rule and reign with Him for eternity.

Joseph had a second son, *"And the name of the second he called Ephraim: 'For God has caused me to be fruitful in the land of my affliction.'"* (Genesis 41:52). The name *Ephraim* means "double ash heap" but can also mean "double fruitfulness." God took the ashes of Joseph's life and made it doubly fruitful because Joseph persevered to come into the presence of God's glory. All the glory that God bestowed on him through Pharaoh did not cause Joseph to stumble. He did not develop a proud or haughty attitude that would have corrupted him and hindered him from fulfilling God's purposes. His God-conscious faith kept him focused on God's glory and not on how God had exalted him. The more we allow God to be manifest in our lives, the more we will be able to relate to God's glory.

When we relate to God's Glory, we no longer view the past difficulties and struggles in our lives with sorrow or disappointment—the veil is removed from our spiritual eyes and our hearts are filled with awe as we recognize the hand of the Master Potter shaping us through every experience. Even in the times we felt alone or abandoned—perhaps even like hopeless failures—God the Master Potter was there—carefully, lovingly, and meticulously working in our hearts, softening us and shaping us into vessels of glory.

As Joseph assumed the position that God had always intended for him—ruler of Egypt and savior of Israel—he looked back at the events of his life—the painful betrayal by his brothers, the agony of being separated from his family, the humiliation of enslavement in Potiphar's house, the injustice of false accusations by Potiphar's wife, years of hopeless captivity as a prisoner, and disappointment as Pharaoh's butler forgot him. Joseph no longer saw a series of tragic, heartbreaking events; instead he regarded his trials as friends and not intruders. Joseph saw God's divine purpose for all the trials he had not only endured but also prospered through as the hand of the potter shaped him for God's purpose. Joseph had learned to trust God in adversity, and to acknowledge and recognize God's hand in the midst of that adversity. As Joseph sat on his throne in one of the most powerful nations in the world at that time, he looked back and could say, *"God has made me forget all my toil and all my father's house"* and *"God has caused me to be fruitful in the land of my affliction."* The vessel was complete. It had passed each step and had come through the fire of God's glory—intact and fully prepared for the Master's use.

THE GLORY OF GOD REVEALED

Our seventh essential relationship with God deals with His glory and the overall test we must pass is the faith test. There are four aspects of God's glory and our faith is tested in each aspect.

CREATIVE FAITH

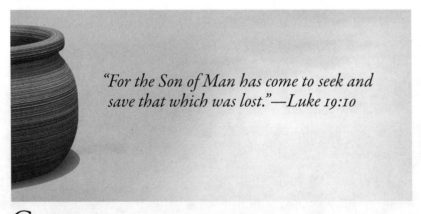

"For the Son of Man has come to seek and save that which was lost."—Luke 19:10

Creative faith can be observed when someone is healed or a miraculous event takes place, but it is also evident when we pray in faith and see God answer our prayers. Creative faith releases the power of God in our lives.

The following story illustrates how the prayers of one man affected the lives of an entire family and is a clear example of creative faith: Robert Ewing began to visit London, Ontario where my family lives in the mid-1970s. His purpose for coming was to encourage some young believers who lived in London. One morning while he was meeting with three Christian young men in one of their apartments, Robert looked out the window at some apartment buildings and told them that the Lord had just instructed him to pray for the family that owned those buildings. He had no idea who the people were for whom he was to pray, but our family owned those buildings. It was at about that same time that my brother and I received Christ as our Savior. Robert did not know us and we did not know Robert.

Years passed and in 1990 my brother, Harvey, met a Jewish believer from Israel, Ilan Zamir, who at that time lived in London. They became good friends. One day Ilan asked Harvey if he wanted to drive to the airport with him to pick up a friend who was coming to visit. That friend was Robert Ewing. Robert had never met my brother and had never heard of him. At the airport Harvey met Robert for the very first time, and greeted him with a very respectful, "It's a pleasure to meet you, Mr. Ewing." Robert responded, "How is your father? I have been praying for him for many years." Understandably my brother was quite surprised by his response. As they met that day, Robert was already seeing a portion of the fruit his many years of prayer for our family had produced. This was the beginning of our relationship with Robert.

The Lord loves to reveal His sovereign hand to us in the most interesting and surprising ways. About five years after we met Robert, my sister and her husband, who are also believers in Christ, were attending a wedding in another city. As they sat around the table my sister began to share the testimony about how Robert had prayed for us for fifteen years before he ever met us. As she shared, one man looked at her and said, "This story sounds familiar." He asked the man's name. When she told him his name was Robert Ewing, the man's eyes grew wide and he said, "I know Robert Ewing. I was one of the three young men in the apartment that morning when the Lord instructed Robert to pray for your family." Now everyone was really excited!

The next week the man drove to London to attend a Bible study being held in our home. He shared his testimony—how he had been with Robert Ewing twenty years earlier when he had begun to pray for our family. As he shared his testimony, another man in the room began to get excited. The second man said, "I was also there twenty years ago." Two of the men who were in that apartment when Robert had begun to pray for our family found themselves again in each other's presence, this time in our home that evening, testifying to God's great faithfulness. The third man who had been privy to the original prayer for our family had moved back to Kenya many years before.

Here is a wonderful example of creative faith being released in my family because God instructed Robert to pray. He was both obedient and faithful to do so—for the following fifteen years he did just that— he prayed for our family— people whose names he did not even know.

Another testimony of creative faith comes from a good friend of mine, Bill Woods, who with his wife, Tammy, are missionaries in southern Mexico. About seven years ago Bill and Tammy felt the Lord calling them to a remote part of Mexico known to be quite hostile to the Gospel. Without much fluency in Spanish, this couple moved to that area, spending the first few months in language school to learn to communicate. They had the support of their local church in the United States and had been sent out with apostolic oversight, but at that time they had no helpers and were basically on their own. It was on their heart to begin a church, an orphanage, and a Bible school. Now after seven years they have an orphanage where they care for about 18 children—that number is still growing—a Bible school with lessons every Saturday morning where leaders are trained, and a vibrant, fast growing church of nearly three hundred people. This introduction itself is an example of creative faith at work.

The illustration I want to focus on in describing creative faith occurred on one of Bill and Tammy's trips back to the United States. During their time in Stillwater, Oklahoma, Bill and Tammy spent time with a Latin American couple. Francisco was from Cuba and his wife from Venezuela. They had recently received the Lord as their Savior. Francisco was a "dumpster diver," who frequented dumpsters on construction sites and behind large stores to search for anything he might find useful. He was forever finding trash—or what appeared to be trash—and making something from it. Francisco invited Bill and Tammy to accompany him and his wife to a Saturday auction where they would be selling used building materials and appliances. Bill agreed although Tammy wasn't too enthusiastic about spending hours watching men doing what they do best—buying hardware—but she agreed.

Saturday came and they arrived at the auction which was held in a huge abandoned supermarket. When they stepped in the door they couldn't believe their eyes—the aisles were stacked with boxes and pallets with everything imaginable waiting to be sold. After about an hour, Tammy was ready to leave but Francisco asked them to wait because he wanted to bid on a large pallet of electrical supplies. His bid was successful and he and Bill began to shuttle the pallet's contents to his pickup truck.

On one of Bill's trips to the pickup he noticed a group of people on their hands and knees looking for something. He thought perhaps someone had lost a contact lens. Bill thought to himself, *never in a million years are they going to find it*; first, because it's small and transparent and second, the floor was so dirty that even if they found it, it would be useless. He asked what they were looking for and a woman looked up with tears in her eyes and said, "I lost my diamond from its Tiffany setting. It's a three carat stone." As Bill heard those words, he again thought they'd never find it because she was the auctioneer's assistant, the person who reached into every box to display the items for sale. She had been assisting for over an hour and many of the purchases had already been removed from the building by their new owners. Quite likely someone would be *very* happy when they arrived home that evening!

Bill continued to shuttle his friend's purchases to his truck and again he saw the group looking for the diamond. This time he sent up a quick prayer, *"Lord, where is that diamond?"* Just as he passed a pallet full of extension cords, the Lord spoke these words to him, "It's in that box." Bill stopped, turned on his heel, and without a second thought began to remove the cords from the box one by one. When Bill removed the last cord, he stared at the bottom of the box. It was full of dirt and debris, but something caught his attention. He noticed what looked like a piece of broken glass—the sort one sees when a windshield breaks. He reached down and picked it up—it was the woman's three carat diamond—God knew it was there all along!

By this time, the woman had stopped searching for her diamond and was crying. Bill felt he should let her know how much God loved her. "Jesus really loves you," he said. As she turned and looked at him, her expression said, "Are you crazy! Can't you see I just lost something very precious?" So he repeated, "You don't understand how much Jesus loves you," and handed her the diamond—which dramatically changed her perception of Bill. The crowd turned and asked Tammy how they found the diamond. (Some people still think that men are incapable of finding anything.) Tammy answered, "We prayed." At that point the auctioneer announced that the diamond was found and they were about to give Bill and Tammy a big round of applause when Tammy shouted, "No! We did nothing. It was Jesus! He showed us where it was." On that note the auctioneer turned around and went back to selling.

The first time Bill shared this testimony with me, his comment was, "Sometimes we think, 'I can't believe God could do this,' but other times we think 'I can't believe God actually did this.'" Even after several years Bill remembers the event clearly and is still awed by what God did. This is a wonderful example of creative faith. Bill made a simple request of the Lord and immediately the Lord spoke to him. *Without hesitation* he acted by faith and searched the box the Lord had indicated. He did not allow doubt or fear of appearing foolish to hinder him from acting on his faith. Through his simple act of obedience motivated by faith, he was able to experience the awesomeness of God's faithfulness. Even the crowd that gathered acknowledged they had witnessed a miracle.

We also see the result of creative faith—the Glory of His Name. Both Bill and Tammy were able to give a clear witness of the love of God and demonstrate in a tangible way His reality and faithfulness. The creative faith seen in this testimony may not appear at first glance to be as dramatic as someone being healed or a limb restored. But as Bill acted on the word of knowledge received from the Holy Spirit, God was able to change the atmosphere in the woman's heart from sorrow to joy in an instant of time. God's creativity invaded the situation to reveal a glimpse of His glory to the woman and those around her.

DOCTRINAL FAITH

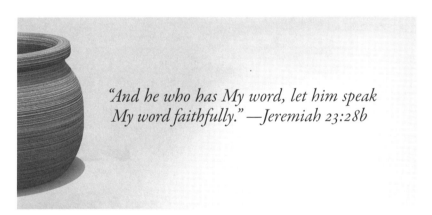

"And he who has My word, let him speak My word faithfully." —Jeremiah 23:28b

The second portion of this testimony illustrates doctrinal faith. About two weeks after the first incident, Bill was driving back from Tulsa, Oklahoma when the Lord spoke to him and said that He wasn't finished with the woman. He told Bill to contact her and tell her that what had happened to the diamond was prophetically significant. God wanted her to know that even as the diamond symbolized her marriage, He was warning her that she was about to lose her marriage. But if she sought Him, He would restore her marriage just as He restored her diamond.

When Bill arrived home, he had no idea how to contact her because he didn't know her name. He called the auction house and they were able to put him in touch with the woman's sister. In a call to the sister, Bill explained about the diamond and the message he felt God wanted him to give her sister. The sister was a Christian and confirmed the trouble in her sister's marriage. Her sister had at one time been involved in church life but something had happened and she stopped attending. After Bill hung up, he immediately called the woman who lost the diamond. She told him that everyone was still talking about what had happened. He relayed to her the word the Lord had given about her marriage. She denied that her marriage was in crisis. Had Bill not spoken with her sister, he might have doubted that he heard from the Lord. Bill believes the woman was simply too embarrassed to confess the truth to him as a total stranger.

To this day, Bill has no idea how she responded after reflecting on the prophetic message or the subsequent state of her marriage. He does, however, know that the Lord spoke to her clearly.

Just as the Lord gave Joseph the correct interpretation and application of Pharaoh's dream, the Lord gave Bill the correct prophetic meaning of the loss of this woman's diamond together with the response that God expected. Here we see doctrinal faith in action. The Lord gave Bill a *rhema* word for her life. In the Greek New Testament, references to *word* are either *"logos"* or *"rhema,"* and each has a slightly different meaning. *Logos* refers to the written or spoken Word of God (as found in the Scriptures) and *rhema* is the revealed word of God. This can be either a Word of Scripture that comes alive for a believer to apply to a particular situation in their life or it can be the Word of the Lord speaking into a person's heart. Dr. Paul Yonggi Cho says *"rhema is a specific word to a specific person in a specific situation."*

Bill stepped out in faith and acted on the words the Lord gave him. He delivered both messages—that God loved her and what she needed to do to restore her marriage. The normal response might have been one of reluctance to contact a stranger to give a word of correction and exhortation about a very personal matter. However, Bill chose to trust God and be obedient to speak without hesitation.

Through a creative miracle, God had filled the woman's heart with awe as He spoke into a distressing situation, returned her diamond, and told her how much He loved her. This prepared her heart to receive a word of correction and guidance. God's purposes are always redemptive. He returned her diamond and turned her sorrow into joy—and His desire was to do the same with her marriage. God's ability to return her diamond should have given her the impetus and encouragement to believe that He would indeed restore her marriage and her relationship with Him. When we step out in creative faith God meets us there and changes our circumstances.

We can fall into error of doctrine if we modify our beliefs or the expression of our beliefs in order not to offend or anger others. In this day of political correctness, error of doctrine can creep in ever so subtly. There are many issues regarding lifestyle and morality on which the Bible is very clear. However, some have modified their doctrine because of social pressures, and have failed to vocalize what they know is Scriptural, or allowed social pressures to influence them to such an extent that they have changed their beliefs.

Bill gave a word to this woman that spoke of her need to repent and rededicate her life to the Lord for her marriage to be restored. God left no doubt about the ultimate outcome of her marriage if she did nothing—the truth dispelled any deception about the gravity of her situation. The first part of the message that the Lord gave her was "Jesus loves you." But two weeks later, the second part of the message was a warning to her. She had sown to the flesh and the harvest would be the failure of her marriage. Even though God loved her, only her willingness to submit and yield to God in obedience would restore the two most important relationships in her life—her relationship with God and her marriage.

Bill's testimony may appear unfinished, as he does not know how the woman ultimately responded to the word given to her. However, when the Lord gives us a word for someone, we need to guard against two errors of doctrine. We can refuse to give it—fearing we will offend the person—or we can give it and try to pressure the person into the correct response—feeling that we have some responsibility in the outcome of the word delivered.

Another friend of mine, Phil Paxton, shared how the Lord taught him to recognize and respect the boundaries of his prophetic ministry. While he was at home one day the door bell rang. When he opened the door, there stood a courier with a package for him. He signed for it and the courier left. Then the Lord spoke to his heart and said, "I want you to be like that courier." At first Phil did not understand. Then the Lord continued, "After the courier delivered the package he did not wait around to see if you would open it but simply left after completing his job. His job was to verify who you were, and give you the package. When I give you a word for someone you are simply to give it. You are not responsible for their response." Bill had delivered God's message to this woman, but how she chose to respond was solely her decision.

Bill was faithful to His responsibility before the Lord and was obedient to the Scriptural principal of exhorting and admonishing. He spoke of her need for repentance which may seem to many as intruding into her personal space. Bill spoke a number of truths from Scripture. First, despite what many believe about divorce and remarriage, marriage is sacred and it was God's intention to restore her marriage. Second, her backsliding had lead to her present difficulties. Third, the only solution to true restoration was to repent and turn back to God. Fourth, God was faithful and if she would humble herself and obey, He would restore her marriage just as surely as He restored her diamond.

PERSEVERING FAITH

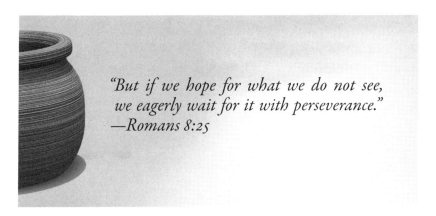

"But if we hope for what we do not see, we eagerly wait for it with perseverance."
—*Romans 8:25*

The third aspect of God's glory is the glory of His life and the test we must pass is the persevering faith test. The danger we must avoid in relationship to this test is error of lifestyle.

Creative faith and doctrinal faith prepare us for persevering faith to come forth. Sometimes persevering faith can be summed up in a person's life in a very few sentences. It seems so easy to say, "Abraham believed God." But Abraham truly persevered in believing God. Seemingly endless years passed between God's promise of a son being born to Abraham and Sarah and the fulfillment of that promise. We need to understand what Abraham experienced during those intervening years to fully grasp the power of that statement. During those long years of waiting he experienced relentless temptation to become disheartened and give up.

A beautiful example of persevering faith can be seen in my mother-in-law's life. Her testimony is one filled with both adventure and hardship. I would like to provide you with a small glimpse of how persevering faith was manifested in her life.

She was born in China of Russian parents. (I jokingly tell people that my mother-in-law is Chinese and watch as they look at my wife in surprise and shock.) Although my mother-in-law was born in China, her spiritual heritage really began in Russia. About 1925, the Pentecostal movement was birthed in Russia. Many people were saved, filled with the Spirit, and the gifts of the Holy Spirit were operating. The Lord began to speak to numbers of Christians throughout Russia that He wanted to take them out of Russia into China. Pockets of believers living all over the Soviet Union received the same message. Those who heard, believed, and acted on the prophetic words, beginning to move closer and closer to the Chinese border.

By 1930, a group of Russian Christians representing many cities in the Soviet Union gathered at a town close to the Chinese border. They rented a building in which to conduct their church meetings. They were careful to maintain a low profile. After they had been there a number of months, one day at a prayer meeting, the Lord spoke prophetically and told them the exact date they were to leave Russia and cross into China. Of course, in the natural, leaving Russia was impossible because the border was heavily guarded. But the Lord provided details as to how to prepare for their journey. Over the next few days, they were instructed to bring luggage into their church building, gradually, so as not to be noticed or draw attention to themselves. They were to take only as much luggage and food as they could comfortably carry with them on their trip.

On the day that the Lord had prescribed, all the families met in the church as if to attend a regular evening church service. Everyone attended from the oldest adult to the youngest child. That night they began to pray and seek the Lord for further direction. Again the Lord spoke prophetically—they were to sit and wait. As evening drew into night, the children fell sleep, but the adults continued to pray. Sometime after midnight, there was an abrupt change in the weather—a very severe storm began. Heavy rain pelted down accompanied by crashing thunder and bolt after bolt of lightening. The intense rain reduced visibility to almost zero. Just then the Lord spoke prophetically, "Go and leave the building." The Lord told them that they were to walk together as families and hold onto the children—and everyone was to hold onto one another. As they left the building, the torrential rains continued.

They walked slowly toward the Chinese border, which was only a short distance away. The actual border between Russia and China was a river. The border crossing consisted of a bridge with a hut where the border guards *could stand*. When they arrived at the bridge—to their amazement—there were no border guards or guard dogs. Both the guards and their dogs had taken shelter in the hut and because of the intense rain, the guards were unable to see beyond a few feet. When they came to the bridge, again a prophetic word was given, "Go fast, don't stop, just cross the bridge." They continued to hold hands in single file as they crossed the bridge into China. The guards were unaware of them as they walked right past the border crossing!

After crossing the bridge they continued to walk. Before them was desolate area. They journeyed through this area for about four days until they reached some small villages. Eventually, they settled in one of the cities in that region of China. They secured jobs, began to settle in, and once again waited for the Lord's direction.

There were no Christians in that area, so they established a church. During the years they endured many hardships. They continued to pray and seek God daily. One prophecy that was given from time to time was that the Lord was going to take them to London. This prophecy was first given in 1925, and several times during the next thirty years. But the prophecy brought some confusion. If their destination was England, they should have been moving closer to Western Europe—not in the opposite direction.

One day when they heard that prophecy someone began to ponder what it meant—that they were going to live in London. That person took out a map of the world. As he looked at it, trying to make sense of what the Lord was saying, he noticed the country of Canada and in total surprise he saw the word LONDON. There was a London in Canada! But that still did not explain how they were going to get there.

During the next twenty-five years, they continued to live in the same city in China. They experienced many hardships and trials through those years. The Chinese government imprisoned some of the Christians, and they experienced natural disasters such as a two-year famine. But in every situation, the Lord spoke prophetically to prepare them for what lay ahead. Sometimes their circumstances seemed impossible, but the Lord continued to reassure them, and every time He proved Himself faithful.

During their last two years in China, the Holy Spirit instructed them to move to Shanghai. Once in Shanghai, they applied for permission to leave China as the Lord had instructed them. The Chinese government told them they would never be granted permission to leave China. However, as they continued to pray, the Lord continued to encourage them not to worry or fear, but to know that He would surely take them out of China.

For two years they waited for the Lord to open the door to leave China. One day a member of the Chinese secret police came to their home. They were unaware at the time that in his pocket was their visa to leave China and travel to Hong Kong. He was very rough with them, taunted them, and told them they would never leave Chinese soil. He wanted them to return to the part of China where they had originally lived. However, their response was, "Jesus will take us out of China." Slamming the door as he left he said, "Then let your Jesus do that." They continued to pray. The next day he returned but he was a changed man. He was polite and spoke to them in a friendly tone, handed them their visas and wished them well. They were on their way to Hong Kong! From Hong Kong, a Christian church in Australia sponsored them to immigrate to Australia. They spent seven years in Australia until a church in Canada sponsored them to come to their country in 1965. Guess where the church that sponsored them was located? London, Ontario, Canada!

They spent twenty-five years in China, seven years in Australia, endured times of persecution, famine and uncertainty—but ultimately they arrived in the exact place the Lord had promised to take them. Their faith persevered as they clung to God day by day—and day by day they experienced and saw God's great faithfulness.

On a personal note, I am very thankful for their persevering faith. Because they came to London, Ontario, I met and married my sweetheart Lena. Of course I didn't meet Lena for another fifteen years. God is never in a hurry and He is never late. That may be a good maxim for persevering faith.

GOD-CONSCIOUS FAITH

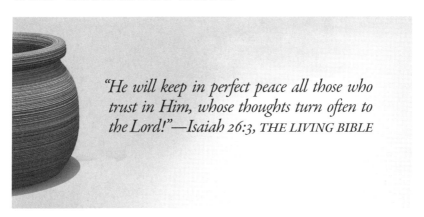

"He will keep in perfect peace all those who trust in Him, whose thoughts turn often to the Lord!"—Isaiah 26:3, THE LIVING BIBLE

The fourth aspect of God's glory is the glory of His presence. The test we must pass is the God-conscious faith test. This is where the reality of God is so great that no matter what we face, the reality of God is greater.

God-conscious faith is the pinnacle of faith because it is birthed in the face of great opposition. It is seen most clearly when a person facing great danger or possible death has confidence in God's abiding presence and sovereignty. It is not simply a feeling, because feelings are fleeting, but it is an aspect of faith carefully developed and matured over years of walking with the Lord.

Creative faith enables us to see the power of God released and this type of faith brings about the Glory of His Name. Doctrinal Faith gives us the correct image of God and the correct foundation on which to build our faith and lifts up the Glory of His Word. Persevering faith carries us through the temptations and tests that try to divert us from the path God has set before us. Persevering Faith manifests the Glory of His Life.

But it is God-conscious faith that exhibits the Glory of His Presence as we face the most severe attacks—physical, emotional, or spiritual— fully confident that the Lord is standing with us. Paul walked in God-conscious faith as he stood alone before the merciless power of the Roman Empire defending the Gospel message. *"At my first defense no one stood with me, but all forsook me. May it not be charged against them. But the Lord stood with me and strengthened me, so that the message might be preached fully through me, and that all the Gentiles might hear. Also I was delivered out of the mouth of the lion."* (2 Timothy 4:16-17).

I experienced an example of God-conscious faith more than twelve years ago. Before I tell this story, I want to make it clear that I do not always walk in this level of God-conscious faith even though that is my desire. It was Saturday, and I had spent the afternoon working on a sermon for the Saturday night youth service.

Shortly after six p.m., just as I was just finishing off the final point, I heard the doorbell ring. My wife answered the door and then I heard her close the door and call down to me, "Come upstairs, there's a drunk outside, you'd better speak to him."

I left my study, went to the front door and as I opened it I saw a man standing there. He was about six-foot-two, about 40 years old, and appeared to be quite strong and muscular. Tattoos of serpents covered his arms. It was evident he had been drinking, but although he was under the influence, it was also evident he was very much in control of himself.

As I stood looking up at him, I said a simple prayer in my heart. *Why is he here Lord?* When we are walking in God-conscious faith, we are aware that God is in control and nothing happens without a purpose. If our circumstances frustrate us, that's a sure sign we are not walking in God-conscious faith. I could have thought, *I have to get ready to go to church and preach a sermon in a few minutes,* but that would be like saying, "God, I don't have time to do Your will because I am too busy at church."

"Hello," I said to him.

He looked at me with blood-shot eyes and said, "Can you help me?"

I stepped outside and over to where, beside the front door, there were two lawn chairs. I closed the front door and we both sat down. He began to tell me about himself and as I carefully listened to him, I was at the same time praying, *Lord, why is he here?* I waited for the voice of the Lord to tell me what He wanted me to do. The man told me he had served five and a half years in prison for robbery. Then he mentioned that sometime in the past he had killed his girlfriend. As he spoke of her death, he broke down and began to cry.

As he continued to tell me about his life, he suddenly stopped and looked rather startled. With an air of suspicion he asked, "Why are you asking me all these questions? Are you going to call the cops on me?"

I responded quietly and said, "No, I just care about you and I want to know a little bit about you. I want you to know a little bit about me too. I'm a born-again Christian."

He looked at me and asked, "What are you going to do—preach at me?"

I answered, without a bit of humor, "No, not unless you want me to."

Then he said, "When I was in prison I accepted Jesus but nothing happened. *Look at my life now!* There is no God." Whether he had truly accepted the Lord I do not know. As we continued to talk I waited on the Lord.

He looked at me, then blurted out, "Well, are you going to help me or not?"

I asked him what he wanted me to do.

He answered, "Can you lend me thirty dollars?"

I said without hesitation, "Sure, I can give you thirty dollars."

He interjected, "No—I just want to borrow it. I'll pay you back."

We only had fifteen dollars in the house. I came back and handed him the money. I told him that was all we had in the house. I offered it to him and he accepted it.

When we sat down again I asked him, "Where are you going to stay tonight?" He had mentioned he was from out of town. I asked him if he wanted me to drive him to the Salvation Army where they have a men's shelter.

Suddenly he sighed, "Drive me down to the cop shop. I'm in big trouble and they're looking for me."

I said "Okay." I went inside and told my wife that I was going to drive him to the police station so he could be taken into custody.

She suggested, "Phone the police and let *them* drive him to the police station."

However, I felt that I needed to drive him. To say she was uncomfortable with my decision would have greatly understated her response.

By now it was nearly seven p.m., so I asked her to call the church and let them know that I would be a little late but that I would still give the message. As I moved toward the door, she looked quite worried. I asked her just to pray and trust that the Lord was in control.

I got into my car with this man and started the engine. Then he asked me if I had a gun. I told him, "No."

Again he said, "I'm in big trouble. They're looking for me."

This time I understood that he was not referring to the police but to other people who were pursuing him. He asked me to drive him to the far side of the city. I told him I would either drive him to the police station or I was going straight to church.

He nodded and said, "Okay, take me to the cop shop."

As I pulled out onto the street, my mind was full of the realization that I was alone in a car with a man who was a wanted criminal and who was apparently capable of extreme violence. Yet I continued to focus on the Lord, to seek His direction and protection, and to maintain my consciousness of His faithfulness. As I began driving down the street, I asked him if I could pray for him.

His response was both immediate and irritated, "It won't help! It won't help!"

I assured him it *would* help but I asked for permission to pray for him. He agreed. As I began to pray for him out loud, he reached over and took hold of my hand. He began to squeeze it. I think he was touched by the prayer and that was his way of responding; he was so strong, however, he was crushing my hand. I continued to pray out loud and seek God's direction for his life.

After I'd driven for about five minutes he said, "Pull over." I pulled the car to the side of the road and as I did he said, "I am sorry but I'm going to have to do this." He repeated it a second time.

I looked at him and said very calmly and clearly, "You are not going to do this because the Lord is with me." My main objective was to speak words of faith and authority. I turned off the car, took my keys out of the ignition, and opened my door to get out of the car.

He asked me what I was doing. I said, "Well, do you want me to take you to the police station or not?"

He shrugged his shoulders and said, "Okay." So I closed the door, started the engine and continued driving.

As we drove down the road, I said to him in a bold voice, "God can change your life!"

He burst out, "No! There is no God. *Look at me! Look at my life!*"

I said, "God didn't do this, you did this to yourself. God *can* change your life. Whether you believe it or not, it is true. I know it is true because I have seen the hand of God change people's lives. He has changed my life." I continued to affirm God's faithfulness as we drove. Finally we arrived at the police station. I stopped the car.

He looked over at me saying, "I don't know how I came to your house. I don't know why I've met you, but I have never met anyone like you before. I believe what you've told me. I believe you." He continued, "We will have to meet some other time. I don't know how and I don't know where." With that he got out of the car.

I have no idea if he went into the police station but I suspect he didn't. I do know that God wanted to convey something to him and if I hadn't been willing to drive him I would never have had the opportunity to speak those words to him. He needed to hear the truth because his heart and mind were so filled with lies.

Not only did the Lord do something in that man's heart but He also did something in my heart. My confidence in the Lord was strengthened through this experience.

I want to make three things abundantly clear about this testimony. First, we must be absolutely sure that we are not moving in presumption, but by the leading of the Holy Spirit. We shouldn't put ourselves at risk in dangerous situations unless we are certain that God is leading us.

Second, even though this story ended peacefully, it does not mean that even if we trust the Lord things will necessarily be easy. While preaching the Gospel or living in dangerous situations, some are miraculously delivered, while others may suffer and die. The Bible says that we will suffer for the Gospel, and there are places in the world where Christians *do* suffer and some die for their faith in Christ. But if they are able to walk in God-conscious faith, then the peace of God that passes all understanding will guard their hearts and minds.

Third, I don't want people to think me more spiritual than I am. Even though I shared an experience where God really sustained me with God-conscious faith, there are still many times that I have failed to trust Him. I still have a great deal of growth ahead of me. However, one thing that I can say for certain: He who has begun a good work in me is faithful to complete it until the day of Jesus Christ. (Philippians 1:6).

Heavenly Father, I thank You that You have called us to be Your children. My heart's cry is that Your glory would fill Your Church and that the full manifestation of the life of Christ and all His glory would be evident in and through the Body of Christ. When Jesus walked on this earth, He said that we will do the things He did—and even greater. Father, lead and protect us that we will not fall into error but cause us to be so dependent upon You that it would not be us who live but Christ who lives through us. Make us into glory containers so that Your glory will shine clearly for all to see. Purify us so that we will in no way oppose what You desire to do. Lord help us yield to You as You take us through these seven essential relationships so that we will not fail to fulfill Your will. Change our hearts from being selfish and self-seeking to hearts that seek only to glorify Jesus. Thank You Lord that You will cause this to happen. Lord let me be one of those who are faithful even unto death. Amen.

OUR RESPONSE

I would encourage you to take a spiritual inventory of your life, to determine where you are in reference to these seven relationships with God. Are you still struggling with obedience to the Word? Are you growing spiritually and moving on in your relationship with Jesus Christ? Most often we will find different levels of maturity in different areas in our lives, and God will often be dealing with several of our seven essential relationships with Him at the same time. For example, we may be submissive to church authority, to governmental authority, but harbor disrespect or even rebellion against our employer at our workplace. We may have a relationship with God's Word and have learned submission. Perhaps our struggle is in refusing to cooperate with God in how He deals with us. We may best relate to Joseph's experience in prison, as he dealt with the bitterness in his heart—those wrong heart attitudes that we would prefer to ignore. Regardless of where we are, such an inventory serves as a spiritual barometer and identifies those areas in our relationship with God that need to be addressed.

Each one of the seven essential relationships is one that God wants to fulfill, manifest, and perfect within every believer. Passing the corresponding test will allow us to fully enter into that relationship with God. He enlarges our capacity for Him through these seven relationships and God will always work on these relationships in His divine order. As our obedience to the Word grows, God will begin to work on our relationship with Him in other areas of our lives.

How should we respond to this teaching? God has engineered every circumstance in our lives for His glory, but it is our choice as to how we respond. Our response to our circumstances is more important than the circumstances themselves. It is often in adverse circumstances that we become aware of issues that prevent us from receiving God's best for our lives. If we are willing, each circumstance can bring about God's purpose in our life—or if we resist—that circumstance can begin to destroy us. Every circumstance, whether a time of joy, sorrow, or heartbreak—is meant to change something in us, whether to cleanse us, purge us, or strengthen us. Each situation has a purpose unique to our personal and unique relationship with God. We need to trust God, and believe that He is in control of our circumstances, working things out for our good if we are responsive to Him.

"And the vessel that he made of clay was marred in the hand of the potter; so he made it again into another vessel, as it seemed good to the potter to make." (Jeremiah 18:4). The vessel that the potter was making was marred because it was not the right kind of clay to produce the vessel he desired. If the clay had not been thoroughly washed, or the hard places softened, he was unable to create the vessel He originally intended. He was forced to remold it into another vessel, one suitable

to the condition of the clay. Because of the poorer quality of the clay, this second vessel would be smaller, and therefore unable to hold as much glory as the potter intended. If we repeatedly resist God as He tries to shape us into His image, He will eventually reform us into an inferior vessel, one with diminished glory.

We need to embrace both the good times and the hard times. Paul understood this very well. Paul knew how to walk through good times and through hardships—he learned to do it through Christ. The purpose of the trials we face is to get to know Jesus more and to depend upon His provision in every circumstance. God has given us the opportunity to take the cup of Christ's sufferings, put it to our lips and taste of it—just a drop—to develop a greater appreciation of Jesus Christ. Becoming partakers of His suffering does a special work in our lives and causes us to identify with the cross and with His sacrifice for us.

Why are all believers not experiencing victory? Are we not all destined to be overcomers? We need to receive and maintain our first love for Jesus. The Church at Ephesus had good works, they were pressing on, they were patient and steadfast, but they lacked one thing—their first love. This should be our number one priority. It may seem easier for us to do works for God than to sit before the Lord in prayer and worship. It is natural if we want to please someone, that our desire will be to do things for them, but if we truly love them, we will want to spend time with them.

These seven relationships are meant to bring forth that first love in us that we may be centered in Christ. If we have that first love, we will be empowered to walk through even our trials with joy.

"And I am certain that God, who began the good work within you, will continue his work until it is finally finished on the day when Christ Jesus returns."
—*Philippians 1:6,* NLT

INVITATION TO SALVATION

Many reading this book will be spirit-filled believers but this may not be so with every reader. Perhaps as you have read this book, you have felt the Lord stirring your heart, and birthing a desire within you to have a personal relationship with God through His Son, Jesus Christ.

You may believe in God—attend religious services or rituals—even pray, yet lack the assurance that your sins have been forgiven. You may come from a Christian background and have been confirmed, dedicated to the Lord—even baptized—maybe you have attended church all your life, yet do not feel you know the Lord Jesus in an intimate way. Perhaps you cannot recall a time when you gave your heart to the Lord and invited Him to be your personal Savior.

Then this prayer is for you...

Heavenly Father, I confess before You that I am a sinner and cannot save myself. I recognize that my sin has separated me from You and Your plan for my life. Thank you for sending Your Son, Jesus Christ, who took upon Himself all of my sins, died in my place on a cross, and was resurrected from the dead. I ask You now to forgive me of all my sins and wash me with the precious blood of Jesus. I invite You to come into my life and make me the person You created me to be, that I may serve You and bring glory to Your name. I thank You and praise You that I am now Your child. In Jesus' name I pray. Amen.

Ask the Lord to lead you to a local Bible-believing church where you can be fed the Word of God to help you grow spiritually. Begin to feed your spirit and soul with the Word of God. Partake in water baptism, as an outward sign that you have received the Lord Jesus Christ, that your former life has passed away, and that you are a new creation. Petition God to bring other Christians into your life who can nurture you and with whom you can have fellowship.

May the Lord bless you in your new life in Christ!

Howard Katz

The Seven Essential Relationships and their corresponding tests are summarized below:

RELATIONSHIP	TEST
With the Word of God	Obedience Test
With the World	Separation Test
With Authority	Submission Test
With How God Deals With Us	Preparation Test
With God's Plan	Possessive Test
With God Himself	Priority Test
	1) The Rest Test
	2) The Faithfulness to the Vision Test
	3) The Grace Test
With God's Glory	Faith Test
	1) Creative Faith Test
	2) Doctrinal Faith Test
	3) Persevering Faith Test
	4) God-Conscious Faith Test

The table below summarizes the glory of God revealed, the faith test and the possible error accompanying each test.

THE GLORY REVEALED	THE FAITH TEST	POSSIBLE ERROR
Glory of God's Word	Creative Faith	Error of Vision
Glory of God's Name	Doctrinal Faith	Error of Doctrine
Glory of God's Life	Persevering Faith	Error of Lifestyle
Glory of God's Presence	God-Conscious Faith	Error of Attitude

Also available from Believe Books:

Will Vaus

MY FATHER WAS A GANGSTER
The Jim Vaus Story

One of the most fascinating conversion stories of the 20th century—the dramatic life story of Jim Vaus, former associate to America's underworld.

Mary Haskett

REVEREND MOTHER'S DAUGHTER
A Real Life Story

In this gripping account, the author shares her personal story of racial rejection, physical and sexual abuse, and wartime trauma. Through it all, she is aware of a driving force in her life that ultimately brings her to Jesus Christ.

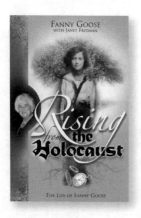

Fanny Goose
with Janet Fridman

RISING FROM THE HOLOCAUST
The Life of Fanny Goose

The astonishing real life story of an indomitable young Jewish girl who miraculously survives the horrors of Hitler's plot to destroy her people and goes on to live a joyful life.

Also available from Believe Books:

Major General Jerry R. Curry

FROM PRIVATE TO GENERAL
*An African American Soldier
Rises Through the Ranks*

Major General Jerry Curry vividly describes his life journey of military missions, powerful positions, and his relationship with the true source of authority—his Father in heaven.

Charlene Curry

THE GENERAL'S LADY
God's Faithfulness to a Military Spouse

Charlene Curry recounts all the joys and challenges of being a career military spouse and how she triumphed over difficulties by relying on a source of spiritual power that transformed her life.

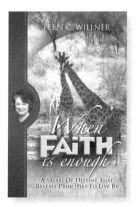

Fern C. Willner

WHEN FAITH IS ENOUGH
*A Safari of Destiny that Reveals
Principles to Live By*

A faith-inspiring story of a missionary wife and mother of seven relying completely on God in the heart of Africa.

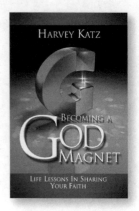

Harvey Katz

BECOMING A GOD MAGNET
The Secret to Sharing Your Faith
Book and **Study & Discussion Guide**

Harvey Katz's book *Becoming a God Magnet* is a practical, effective guide to evangelism. The *Study & Discussion Guide* is ideal for church or home groups willing to learn and share successful methods of personal evangelism.

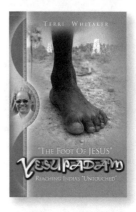

Terri Whitaker

YESUPADAM
Reaching India's Untouched

Yesupadam is the amazing story of God's miraculous work through an Untouchable Indian believer in Jesus and his Love-n-Care ministry in eastern India.

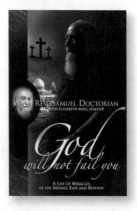

Rev. Samuel Doctorian
with Elizabeth Moll Stalcup, Ph.D.

GOD WILL NOT FAIL YOU
A Life of Miracles in the Middle East and Beyond

The miraculous life story of Rev. Samuel Doctorian, the renowned evangelist used mightily by God in the Middle East and around the world.